SONGS FROM MY HEART

The Stories Behind the Songs

SONGS
FROM MY
HEART
~ *The Stories Behind the Songs* ~

JANICE KAPP PERRY

Sounds
—OF—
ZION
INCORPORATED

Sounds of Zion, Inc. • 9298 South 500 West • Sandy UT 84070-2536

ISBN 1-886472-65-3

First Printing August 2000

ACKNOWLEDGMENTS

I wish to express heartfelt thanks to

My son John, who is the arms, hands, and heart of every project I undertake, be it typing, design, formatting, advertising, printing, or distribution.

Our publisher, Doyl Peck, of Sounds of Zion, for the confidence to publish this book and for almost two decades of comfortable business dealings and friendship.

My friend Suzanne Brady, the sweet little girl I tended in the 50s, who provided much needed encouragement and support in this project of the heart.

And to my husband, Douglas Colton Perry, who makes me feel capable, supports and encourages my creative impulses, and gently pushes me beyond my comfort zone to worthwhile achievements.

–Janice Perry

CONTENTS

FOREWORD

*N*early everyone in The Church of Jesus Christ of Latter-day Saints has sung the songs of Janice Kapp Perry, but not everyone realizes it. Relief Society sisters worldwide unite as they sing "As Sisters in Zion" from the hymnbook. Missionaries in all parts of the world are fortified as they fervently sing the song they learned in Primary, "We'll Bring the World His Truth." Young women more clearly understand their purpose in life as they sing "I Walk by Faith," their Young Women theme song. Primary children express their desire to draw close to their Heavenly Father as they sing "A Child's Prayer," and these are only four of Janice's songs now considered classics in the Church.

This gifted Latter-day Saint composer has written more than seven hundred songs thus far. She has been hailed by some as the most prolific composer of LDS music in the history of the Church, but she will be the last to let you know. Although she has always felt somewhat embarrassed and unworthy of the attention, Janice has received many awards for her musical accomplishments, including the following: Ricks College Exemplary Woman of the Year 1996, Brigham Young University Distinguished Service Alumni 1997 (for her musical contributions and the service she has given to the Church and to her fifteen foster children), LDS Booksellers Lifetime Achievement 1999, and Utah California Women's Utah Heritage Award 1999. Each time I've heard her say, "I feel honored but very uncomfortable standing up in front of people to receive an award." And she means it. Her goal in life is not to be singled out for any contribution or fame but to bless the lives of others through her music.

That is Janice Kapp Perry, humble and filled with a desire to serve and share her talents. It's always been that way with her and her music. We're cousins, and I lived near her on our families' neighboring farms in Vale, Oregon. Her mother, a loving woman with her own amazing musical talent, taught Janice to play the piano from age six to twelve, when she moved on to learn from other teachers. Janice became Primary organist in our ward when she was only twelve years old, and she served in that calling, as well as those of ward organist or chorister, until she went to college. Even then she was gentle and shy when it came to any recognition for her musical talent.

Yet, put her on the pitcher's mound or in the batter's box on the school softball team, and she turned into a fierce competitor dead set on winning the championship and loving every minute of the glory. In those days she might have been more readily pegged as a future all-star sportswoman with a large tally of won games on the scoreboard instead of volumes of musical compositions to her credit.

Little did we know then that instead of applauding her home runs we would be giving her standing ovations in the Tabernacle and other impressive halls in gratitude for her beautiful music. Nor did any of us know then that on a future date she would be honored as nine thousand high school choir students standing in front of the Washington Monument sang "Everyday Heroes," a song she had written with Senator Orrin Hatch. And would we ever have guessed that this avid racquetball player, who conquered most everyone who dared challenge her to a game, would have written forty albums and songbooks, eight sacred cantatas, two musical productions, ten songs in the Primary song book, and one in the hymnbook? But she did, and far more. Would we have guessed in those early years that her songs would be performed by the Mormon Tabernacle Choir, the Mormon Youth Symphony and Chorus, and many other choruses throughout the world? They have been, and who knows what is yet ahead.

A choice thing about her song-writing is that each was written for a purpose beyond herself. Many were written at the request of Church leaders wanting a song for a specific theme. Some were written simply to give comfort to someone who was suffering. Others were written to give guidance to children and youth that they might seek for goodness in their lives and for women and men who needed to feel the loving touch of the Savior through music. Still others were written as an expression of her own testimony. All were written as a legacy of inspiration to her four living children and thirteen grandchildren and as a gift of gratitude to her parents and grandparents. She did it all with only two years of college musical training, a disabled left hand, and a constant reliance upon the Lord for guidance. Her simple style was meant to be so that all might benefit.

When you read her stories behind the songs and then read her lyrics in poetry form, you will see her from a perspective you may never have guessed. Her loving, gentle spirit shows through every story and lyric, and it is then that you come to know the real Janice Kapp Perry, the Latter-day Saint musical phenomenon of our time.

– Joy Saunders Lundberg

Coauthor of *I Don't Have to Make Everything All Better*

-One-

MY BEGINNINGS

$\mathcal{M}$y childhood home was always filled with happy music. Mother said I could play tunes by ear on the piano when I was two years old. She thought that was remarkable, but she thought everything her children did was remarkable. Her enthusiasm for our accomplishments at every age gave us a certain confidence that we had special abilities. Being taught to believe in yourself is a priceless gift indeed.

My mother, Ruth Saunders Kapp, was my main piano teacher through the years, though I studied briefly with other teachers. I wouldn't describe myself as a serious piano student, because my interests were strongly divided between music and sports. It is probably more accurate to describe myself as an adequate accompanist and ward organist rather than as a confident or accomplished soloist.

During my early years, my father, Jacob Kapp, worked as a salesman for a wholesale drug company and then as a carpenter at Clearfield Naval Base in northern Utah. He also raised mink. I was his shadow, following him everywhere, wearing my hair in *stittens* (Dutch dialect for "braids") to please him. From the first, I was tomboyish and uninterested in feminine frills (that has never changed).

After my baptism at age eight, our family, along with two other relatives' families, moved from the city of my birth, Ogden, Utah, to the farming community of Vale, Oregon. There my parents raised crops, milked cows, suffered the financial reverses typical of farmers, and provided us with a loving, secure, gospel-centered home.

Because I attended grade school, junior high, and high school in Vale, that seems to be where I am from. That small community with a high proportion of Church members was a wonderful

place to grow up, yet I know my parents faced some very difficult financial struggles there. It was a guessing game for the farmers. When the price of potatoes was high, we had raised hay; when the price of sugar beets was high, we had raised potatoes; when we raised white-faced cattle, the price of beef dropped—one year twenty steers died from shipping fever. The list goes on. And yet despite these difficulties, my memories of home during these times are very sweet—an overriding happy feeling about my childhood home, the love of my family and friends, and fun through music and sports.

I loved our Vale ward, where I served as organist or chorister for five or six years before college. I conducted the congregation in singing "We Thank Thee, Oh God, for a Prophet" with our prophet, President David O. McKay, in attendance—a never-to-be-forgotten experience.

Mother was a wonderful musician. In her lifetime she wrote, directed, and accompanied some fifteen outstanding roadshows in which the youth found themselves acting, dancing, and singing almost beyond their ability. She also wrote and produced other shows, including a popular minstrel show in which Dad sang the part of Al Jolson. She did much to develop talents in our ward, and we, her family, benefited greatly.

One of the real institutions in Vale and surrounding areas was the Kapp Orchestra. Mother played piano and Dad played drums in a four-piece dance band for almost every church and community dance in the area for twenty years. There was a dance at the church nearly every week, at which people of all ages danced together and had a marvelous time. I did all my high school dating and dancing to the rhythm of the Kapp Orchestra, with Mom and Dad winking and smiling at me each time I danced by. I have not heard the kind of happy, toe-tapping rhythm they provided since they retired their band upon moving back to Utah in their later years.

In high school I had great fun playing percussion instruments, particularly snare drum and tympani, in the school band. A highlight of my senior year was performing dramatic tympani solos at two different concerts: *Concerto for Tympani,* by Jaromir Weinberger, and *Tympendium,* by Schinstine, accompanied by a brass choir. Kettle drums, or tympani, were new to our small community and, supported by a brass choir, were quite electrifying.

I often sang in trios and duets with friends during my teenage years and accompanied other friends on the piano. Every Saturday morning I played piano for Grace's School of Dance for tap and ballet students—my first earnings. During my senior year a few friends and I (on piano) formed a dance band that played for school dances.

As a senior in high school I remember a friend saying, "I don't see how *anyone* could write new music!" Her statement caused me some serious reflection because I had always assumed anyone could if he or she wanted to. Thus, I set out to "write music," deciding on a women's trio with descant. I entitled this first attempt "I Walked in God's Garden," wrote the words first, the parts second, and the accompaniment last. My friends sang it with me in church. It seemed to be well received, and I filed it away, convinced that I could write music. I happened to come across that piece a few years later after taking two years of classes in music theory and composition at BYU and was surprised at how well I had followed the rules of music theory before I really knew them. For me, writing music seems as much instinctive as learned—though surely both are important.

I had another interest that overshadowed even my keen interest in music—an almost fanatical interest in sports. My brother Jack, who was four years older than I, was devoted to high school athletics, and because he needed someone to practice with out on the farm, he groomed me as his practice partner. He showed me no mercy and teased and chided me when I couldn't take what he dished out. At times I would cry out when his fast pitches stung my hand. When that happened he would threaten that if I told Mom and Dad, he would throw harder next time—or maybe not practice with me at all any more. Oddly enough, I wanted to play with him so badly that I didn't tell on him despite many serious sprains and chips and blisters. I don't think I ever proved myself to him, but when I began playing on church and city teams myself, I could see that what he had taught me helped a lot. For instance, Jack had mounted a car tire on our red barn to represent the strike zone and showed me how to fast pitch. Hundreds of hours of practicing gave me a skill that I enjoyed immensely until age forty, feeling grateful for all he had taught me in the school of hard knocks. Farming communities usually take their sports seriously, and through my growing-up years I *lived* to play softball, volleyball, basketball, and sometimes even football.

My summers through high school and afterward were spent working in the potato sheds and the Ore-Ida frozen foods factory. Dad said, "Why don't you give piano lessons instead?" I told him I liked a physical job and would not like giving piano lessons. He had always enjoyed hearing me play the piano and had been willing to pay for my lessons, but now, remembering all the money he had put into my musical training, he said, "Well, then, what are you going to *do* with your music?" I just said, "I don't know yet, Dad, but I promise I'll do something."

I had the feeling through high school that I should decide between sports and music and then devote myself to excelling in one or the other. But I never really resolved that situation. At the end of my senior year I was president of the Girls Athletic Association and received the outstanding music student award.

I graduated from high school as salutatorian and immediately returned to Ogden, Utah, to live with my grandparents. There I worked in the office and played the organ at an uncle's mortuary. I pitched for an Ogden City women's softball team and had a very exciting summer playing ball. I also fell in love and became engaged to be married, but my father received some inspiration that caused me to break the engagement and enroll at Brigham Young University.

Though I still found many opportunities to play ball, I majored in music education at Brigham Young University for two years, from 1956 to 1958. I particularly enjoyed the music-theory writing assignments. I suppose a key to discovering our individual talents is to notice what comes easy and natural to us or even what seems familiar to us. Perhaps these talents that seem so familiar came with us as we began our mortal existence, and the fleeting feelings of familiarity are subtle reminders of a premortal experience.

I sent some of my first assignments and experiments in writing piano music home to my sister Annette (Nettie), who at twelve years of age was an accomplished pianist, having been blessed with perfect pitch, an uncanny ability to memorize, and a healthy dose of confidence. Three of these early pieces were "Campus Blues," "Rag-Net," and "Rondo." Some thirty-three years later, in 1989, she returned to Utah from Fairbanks, Alaska, to present a piano concert. As part of her concert, listed on the program as "Early Writings of a Well-Known Composer," she surprised me completely by playing these three pieces with a flair that delighted the audience.

But returning to the story—on the first day of my sophomore year at BYU I met my future husband, Douglas Colton Perry. He had just completed a mission to France, and we had several music classes together, including music theory, concert band, vocal workshop, and woodwind workshop. We had much in common that precipitated a memorable event a few weeks into the semester. Out of the blue, in our clarinet workshop, Doug whispered to me, "Those lips look like they were made for something better than playing the clarinet!" This was the beginning of the end of my college career, and we were married in the Logan Temple on September 24, 1958.

And though we met in music classes, he later confided to me, "Remember our elders quorum picnic where you were playing shortstop? This guy hits a bullet straight at you, you catch it bare-handed and throw to second for a double play—that *really* impressed me!" The fact that he would say that impressed *me!* Not every guy I had dated felt secure with my athletic abilities.

Doug was an accomplished athlete in sports I had never even tried—swimming and skating—and I was always in awe when I saw him perform. Our shared love of sports and music created a bond that has increased through the years.

Doug was in the army for the first three years of our marriage, so I was unable to finish college. We both participated in Church music wherever we were stationed, played ball when possible, and started our family. Our first child, Steven, was born at Fort Ord, California, in 1960.

After being released from the service, Doug and Steven and I returned to BYU, where Doug received his bachelor's degree in Russian. Two more children, Robert and Lynne, were born in Provo. During these years sports seemed to have the upper hand over music as I played on various softball and volleyball teams for the Church and city. These were excellent teams that went as far as you can go in Church competition—a real highlight of my athletic participation.

We had no piano for the first seven years of our marriage. While Doug was going to graduate school at Indiana University, we finally purchased our first piano. But, in addition to playing Church volleyball and city softball, I had discovered racquetball, and every spare minute was spent on the court.

Our son John was born in Indiana, as was our son Richard, who lived only briefly because of Rh-factor complications—a very tender time for our family.

We had hoped to have a larger family, but because Rh complications are progressive with each succeeding birth, our doctor strongly counseled against future pregnancies. I turned with new devotion and appreciation to our four living children—three sons and one daughter. My joy in being a mother had always exceeded any other interest, and I could not bear to have the children in someone else's care while I went to work to supplement our income during Doug's four years in graduate school. So I tended several other children in our home and typed for students and professors at home before the children were awake in the morning and after they had gone to bed at night. It was a struggle in our tiny army barracks apartment, with little income, but Doug and I remember it as a very happy time in our lives.

During our last two years in Indiana we moved to a small rental home in Bloomington, and Doug worked in data processing at Crane Naval Ammunition Depot and later at Westinghouse Corp. Because my father was dying, we moved back to Utah in 1970 to be with the family, and Doug worked in the controller's office at Utah State University.

Doug was consumed by racquetball and became a perennial champion on campus. I played on Church softball and volleyball teams and participated in some of the most exciting tournaments of my life. I also pitched for a city team, Morris Motors, which was a challenge at my maturing age. Our team earned the right to play the Shamrocks, Utah's top semiprofessional women's team, in the state playoffs in Salt Lake City. Standing on the mound to pitch to them was the sports thrill of a lifetime, even though I knew they would beat us, which they did.

I wrote two pieces of music while we lived in Logan, but then I got involved in coaching the city softball team my daughter, Lynne, played on. The time to write was postponed again.

In 1974 we bought a home in Provo, Utah, and Doug commuted to work in Salt Lake City. I had planned to be less active in sports but was asked to organize a women's sports program in our stake. Thus, I continued playing Church ball and racquetball for a few more years. I also pitched for a city team, Suntana Raceway, though at thirty-six I was exactly twice the age of the eighteen-year-olds who made up the rest of the team. I was painfully aware that my reaction time in sports was slowing down and that I was being injured more often. I had naively assumed I would play ball my whole life, and it was a sad realization, as I neared age forty, that I couldn't safely continue to play with the intensity of the past. Little did I know what a change the next chapter in my life would bring.

-Two-

FROM SCOREBOARD TO KEYBOARD

*T*wo lucky "breaks" pointed me in the direction of writing music. First, I broke my ankle during a game of one-on-one basketball with my nephew, and second, our TV broke. With no TV to watch (for eight years, as it turned out), I had more time to do other things. And as for the broken ankle, one evening as I was lying in bed with my foot elevated in a cast, nursing this painful injury, my husband sat on the edge of the bed looking serious and with a little pleading in his eyes. "Honey, this is a serious injury, and there have been many injuries lately. I know how you love to play ball, and I've always wanted you to, but maybe the time has come for you to consider finding something else that would give you fulfillment— something a little safer."

The idea of giving up sports hurt a lot, and I rebelled at the idea at first. But my broken ankle hurt a lot, too, so I grudgingly began to consider a midlife adjustment. There had been a lot of injuries lately, including a line-drive ball to the pitcher's mound that hit me hard in the stomach before I could react (a few years before, I would have caught it), a jammed finger and broken glasses from playing racquetball, and a strained back from sliding into second base. I knew it was time to make a change, but the admission was painful.

The bishop solved the immediate problem of what to do by calling me to write the ward's roadshow. "Original music would give us extra points," he said hopefully. "Why don't you give it a try?"

I protested mildly, saying I wasn't sure I knew how to write music—it had been twenty years since my college attempts. As I considered the idea, however, a kind of subconscious excitement developed. I wasn't sure I could do it, but something inside me whispered that I probably could and it might even be fun. An encouraging phrase from my patriarchal blessing filtered into my mind just at the right moment. So, with pen in hand, a prayer in my heart, and a clumsy cast on my foot, I began to write music for *The Cat That Quacked,* a fifteen-minute musical comedy.

With fifteen winning roadshows under her own belt, Mother was a great cheerleader and kept me believing that I could do it. I felt excitement as the music and lyrics took shape, and when I saw the creations come to life on stage under the direction of an outstanding director and some very capable young people, I was hooked. Winning first place for the roadshow was a cherry on the sundae, but the real prize for me was the direction this simple endeavor gave to my life.

The kids in the roadshow begged me to write more music for them. What to write? I had always loved pop music—wouldn't miss the Saturday evening radio hit parade for anything in my teenage years—so the first idea that came to mind was to write popular songs. I began with a vengeance, writing twelve pop songs in just a few weeks, and giving them such titles as "Soaring," "There Goes the Girl," "Goin' My Way Alone," "The Sunrise of Our Love," and "Tiny Miracles." I had a demo tape made of four of the best and sent them to Los Angeles and Nashville and wherever I could think of. Responses—or lack of responses—made me gradually face reality: there were a million pop song writers out there, and a song writer had to physically go to those places and knock on doors to hope for success. Most recording companies didn't even accept unsolicited demos, and critiques that were returned did nothing to build confidence in my ability.

In a moment of introspection, I asked myself, "Why write pop music, anyway? It's uncomfortable trying to write lyrics the kids will accept without compromising your own standards. It's not worth it to always be walking that fine line." I began to think seriously about what kind of music I did want to write, because I was perfectly sure of one thing: I did want to write music.

One particular day in 1976 stands out in my mind as the exact beginning of my writing more meaningful music. Doug had taken all the kids somewhere for the afternoon, and I found myself in the unusual situation of being home alone for several hours. I sat down to relax and soon found myself pondering my decision about what kind of music to write. A new kind of LDS music was emerging in stage plays at that time, and I felt very drawn to it as a listener. My son Steven was often a participant in these plays, performing in two such productions while still in high school. He was also studying voice seriously and looking for new music to sing.

Feeling the need for direction from the Spirit, I knelt by my piano bench and offered a simple, direct prayer for guidance in my writing. And then, most important of all, I believe, I listened for a long time for the answer. I thought about all the beautiful, simple music in the Church that had touched me so deeply, increasing my understanding and strengthening my testimony. I suddenly had a strong desire to add to that kind of music and specifically to provide uplifting music for my children to sing. I had no aspirations beyond writing for my own family and friends, but that goal was quite enough to motivate me.

I reached for a pencil and paper and prepared to write. The phrase "I'll follow Jesus" came into my mind. I loved the simple directness of that declaration and considered it a good title for my first gospel song. I immediately felt a confirmation that writing about gospel subjects would be a fulfilling pursuit and regretted even the short time I had spent on pop music, although I had learned some valuable lessons in writing lyrics from the critiques I had received.

During the next two hours I wrote the first verse and the chorus. Then I sat at the piano and wrote a simple accompaniment. I played and sang the first verse and chorus over and over, finding unexpected joy in the experience of setting my testimony to music. I'm not sure any song I've written since that night has stirred me quite as much.

I wrote the second and third verses before my family returned home. I asked my audience of five if they would like to come in and hear my first attempt at writing sacred music. Sensing how important the moment was for me, they all filed in and sat quietly as I played "I'll Follow Jesus." Everyone was quiet as I finished. Then Doug put his arms around me, and the tears in his eyes were the greatest encouragement I could have received.

I could hardly sleep that night. I wanted to stay awake and plan other songs. I felt free to write now. Our youngest child was ten years old, and I had at least six hours home alone each day while all the kids were in school and Doug was at work. I could plunge into this new phase of my life wholeheartedly because it was the right season and I knew "that none had been sacrificed at the altar of my own self-expression."[1]

I sent a copy of that first piece, "I'll Follow Jesus," to my brother Jack, knowing how much he loved to sing. He enjoyed the piece and asked why I didn't publish it. Shortly thereafter I saw the tiniest advertisement in the classified section of the paper: "LDS Songwriters—have your music evaluated for publication." Gathering my courage, I made an appointment to play my music for Jerry Jackman and showed up on his doorstep for an audition. Jerry's company, which is highly successful and well-known in LDS circles today, was just getting off the ground at that time. He couldn't publish my music, but his positive response was a significant influence in my decision to publish it on my own. My brother Jack enthusiastically offered to pay the two hundred dollar cost of publication, saying that I would need to repay him only if I recovered the money from sales. My younger brother, Gary, offered his beautiful painting of Jesus with two children as a cover picture. With that kind of support, and nothing to lose, we ventured into publishing our first piece of sheet music.

Seeing the first printed copies come off the press, I was in awe and also a bit apprehensive about putting it before the public. Not many people were writing or publishing LDS music at that time, however, and the bookstores in Utah were willing to give it a try. When the reorders started coming in, I was thrilled!

Happily, I was soon able to repay Jack, and from then on each project seemed to pay for the next one. Things happened quite fast, and soon we had ten published pieces. I had never thought of the income as anything other than a way to finance the next piece or project or help with mission expenses, for we were entering that phase of our lives and weren't sure where our children's mission money would come from.

Writing opportunities began to come my way, especially for Young Women and missionaries. My first song for Young Women was an assigned theme for a stake YW conference—"My Star Is Rising." My first missionary song was a collaboration with a friend from our ward, Monita Turley Robison, for her son's missionary farewell—"In the Hollow of Thy Hand." Another of these early songs was "Where Is Heaven?" the lyrics reflecting some of the thoughts and questions in my mind since the death of our son Richard, who had lived only eight hours.

The next year I was again asked to write the roadshow music, and this time I set out with enthusiasm and a degree of confidence to write *The One and Only New-World Noah's Ark Band,* which to this day is still my favorite of all the roadshows I have ever been involved with. The show did win again, but a wonderful benefit was that Merrill Jenson, a well-known writer and arranger for BYU Motion Picture Studios happened to be the stake roadshow director. In one of our weekly conversations he asked, "Don't you think it's time to produce an album of your published pieces?"

I answered, "I'd love to, but how much would it cost?"

"I think I could produce a first-rate album in Los Angeles for about ten thousand dollars," he replied.

I restrained myself from laughing incredulously at the amount but told him in all honesty it might as well be ten million dollars as far as our ability to pay was concerned.

"There's a way," he said. "Just find ten people who believe in your music, borrow a thousand dollars from each of them, and tell them you'll have it repaid in a year."

We had always been so careful to avoid debt that I almost didn't even consider his suggestion; however, another LDS producer had also offered to produce an album of these songs, and it seemed the time had come to make a decision. I decided to test the waters. I didn't even know for sure whether there *were* ten people who believed in the music enough to risk a thousand dollars. To my amazement, the first five people I approached were, indeed, willing. And when I made the sixth call, to (who else?) my mother, she agreed to finance the remaining five thousand dollars.

Merrill Jenson was soon on his way to Los Angeles with his arrangements in hand for the ten songs for the album *Where Is Heaven*. The instrumental accompaniments were recorded there by fine studio musicians, and he returned to the BYU Recording Studio to add the vocalists. Randy Boothe, director of the BYU Young Ambassadors, helped immensely in choosing vocalists and coaching them in the studio, spending long, hard hours for almost no pay to help us along in this first effort.

Receiving the first record pressings for the album was another first that put me on cloud nine. I'd be embarrassed to admit how many times I played the album that first day, feeling an incredible excitement at hearing the sheet music come to life and also a strong confirmation that it was the right thing to have done.

The album was well received, the investors were soon repaid, and we had a means of supporting our missionaries just in time. Steve was called to the Belgium Antwerp Mission just after this album was released. Robert was soon called to the Korea Seoul Mission, followed by Lynne to the Washington D.C. Mission and John to the Argentina Rosario Mission.

Many others added their musical talents and gospel spirit to the production of subsequent albums. In addition to Merrill and Randy, such talents as Roger Hoffman, Randy Kartchner, Greg Hansen, Steve Perry, Guy and Kristen Randle at Rosewood Recording Company, and many vocalists and instrumentalists have contributed their talents, touch, and spirit to our songs.

I told Doug I wished I'd started writing music sooner, and he said, "No, those first years were your research phase. You were experiencing the things that you can now write about." He was right. We had reared our children. My father had died. One of our children had died. We had reared foster children. All these experiences refined and taught me while my love for music was simmering. For years Doug and I had been focused on getting our children started singing, playing instruments, and even writing music—following their interests. That was the right time for us to do that.

It's a happy situation when life circumstances allow you to spend time doing what you love to do. You feel twice blessed when you know that what you do has the power to uplift or bless others in a significant way. The knowledge that that was happening with the music was a humbling realization, and I felt a great responsibility to produce good, wholesome music with doctrinally correct lyrics and to be sure of my own personal worthiness to receive the Lord's inspiration in my writing.

Note
[1] Millie Foster Cheesman, *Reflections of a Modern Pioneer,* (Provo, Utah: Community Press, 1976) 88.

-*Three*-

MY OWN LITTLE CORNER
OF THE WORLD AND BEYOND

*S*oon after I had written my first batch of songs, I sent them to the Church Music office, hoping the Church would have a use for them. Brother Michael Moody, our Church Music Chairman, kindly advised me to use my music to "brighten my own little corner of the world." I took his advice to heart and wrote many songs for my ward and stake: "I Love to See the Temple," "I'm Trying to Be like Jesus," "Love Is Spoken Here," "We'll Bring the World His Truth"—and if they had only been used in my ward or even just in my home I would have found that very fulfilling. Many unexpected challenges and surprises awaited, however, as I began writing in earnest.

Writing was a consuming hobby, and when one piece was finished, I could scarcely wait to begin the next. I wrote about what was happening in my own life and found that my experiences were common to many LDS families, who were interested in the songs. For instance, the tender feelings of parents saying goodbye to their missionary as expressed in "In the Hollow of Thy Hand" are common to thousands of parents throughout the Church. Author Chaim Potok once said that "from the personal comes the universal," and I found that to be true with my gospel music.

There were also challenges as I began writing. I inexplicably lost control of my left hand, which made it painful and finally impossible to play the piano. This was very difficult emotionally and caused a lot of soul-searching, which in the end humbled me and turned me more toward the Lord and his purposes for me. I finally gave up playing the piano and turned to more writing.

One album followed another, and eventually I cowrote a

full-length musical, *It's a Miracle,* with my cousin Joy Saunders Lundberg. This project took over the lives of her family and mine as we traveled thirty-nine states giving 239 performances over a three-year period. Our goal was to promote missionary service, and it was an exciting time with family members touring and performing with us.

I also cowrote another musical, *The Warm Place,* this one with Val Camenish Wilcox. It was performed in our stake and at Promised Valley Playhouse in Salt Lake City.

As I wrote and published more, the boxes of sheet music, records, and cassettes piled in the hallways pushed us out of our modest home. We moved across town to a larger home that could accommodate our growing music business, for that is what it had become. We hoped each project would do well so we would be able to fund the next one.

Doug left his work to join us in our music engraving, publication and distribution. Our son John eventually became manager of our business, Prime Recordings. Our son Steven and daughter, Lynne, joined us in writing music, and our son Robert has helped in his area of expertise—computers and web design. My brother Gary L. Kapp, well-known for his religious and western paintings, provided cover art for most of our early publications. His wife, Diane Perry Kapp (Doug's sister), input the music for our music publications. The family involvement in our musical projects has been one of the most rewarding aspects of it.

After the first album was recorded, I started receiving requests to speak. I was terrified. I would have played ball in front of anybody, but I didn't know how to stand up and talk about my music. Doug assured me that any woman in the Church can stand up and bear her testimony about what she herself has learned. But for at least two years, I let my fears hold me back. Eventually I risked it. And it was truly scary, start to finish. I had to decide whether to keep speaking publically and overcome my fear, or just quit trying. I kept trying. It took five years for me to overcome my fear of speaking, and still I refused to sing in public. A wise old Hawaiian woman chastised me when I declined to sing a solo at a fireside. Holding back was a sign of pride, she said. Just stand up, do your best, and look to the

Lord for your approval, not the world, she instructed me. I took her advice, and I've been singing ever since. Doug and I have traveled to scores of stakes throughout the Church to share our testimonies of the gospel in a musical way. It has been a wonderful way to collect new friends and share our musical mission.

So many wonderful things happened for us during the next few years that were related to music—things that far exceeded any aspirations I had when I began writing. For a few years I felt especially moved upon to write and record children's music. I understood that prompting years later when ten of these songs were included in the *Children's Songbook,* published by the Church. I was also given an opportunity, by the Church Music Department, to provide a hymn setting for Emily Woodmansee's beautiful text "As Sisters in Zion," which appears in the LDS hymnbook. I experienced a unique outpouring of the Spirit as I wrote songs for the Young Women values, especially "I Walk by Faith."

I was delighted when on two separate occasions the Mormon Youth Symphony and Chorus performed in the Salt Lake Tabernacle two sacred Easter cantatas I had cowritten with Joy Lundberg. Eventually several of my compositions were even sung by the Mormon Tabernacle Choir during my tenure in the Choir—an unbelievable thrill.

I had never planned to audition for the Tabernacle Choir, feeling quite sure that I was too weak vocally. Then one day, while waiting in a doctor's office, I read a brief article called "Feeling the Fear but Doing It Anyway." Challenge yourself, the article suggested, to do something way beyond your abilities, and see how far you get. Any little distance you cover will be a victory. I told Doug about the article, and he suggested that I try out for the Tabernacle Choir. I nearly fell off my chair. That *was* out of reach, something I'd never even considered. But I asked around and learned that try-outs included three parts. First was a written test. I took it, and I passed. Then they required a home demo tape. I did that, and I passed. Next was a personal audition—when there was an opening. After waiting two and a half years, I wrote in my journal, "I tried out for the Tabernacle

Choir. I made it two-thirds of the way, and that was a victory."
I closed that chapter.

Two weeks later, I received a call inviting me to a personal audition. Talk about fear! "You'll always wonder if you don't try," Doug said. I was fifty-five. Choir members generally aren't accepted after age fifty-five because members have to quit at sixty, and they like you to serve for five years. Doug went with me to the audition. The person before me had the most exquisite, well-trained voice. I said, "Doug, let's go before she comes out. I cannot do this." The door opened. Doug took my hand and pulled me into the audition room. I had never known fear like that. As I sang my audition, I thought, *Whose voice is this anyway? It's not mine.* I knew I had not done my best.

Afterwards I cried all evening, certain I would never sing in the Tabernacle Choir. Two weeks later, to my amazement, I received a call to sing in the Choir. Sister JoAnn Ottley, who worked with new Choir members who needed a little extra vocal help, called me in right away. I said, "Sister Ottley, when I auditioned, I was too afraid even to do what I can do. For my peace of mind, tell me, how did I get into the Choir?" She answered, "Well, we could tell you were afraid. We knew your musical background from your written test, and we had heard your tape. But sometimes we hear a voice that won't *hurt* the choir, and we feel we can bring you along with us." She paused a moment and then smiled. "The bottom line is we pray over every person who auditions, and if the Lord says yes, you're called. So work hard, and be at peace."

Of all my experiences with the Tabernacle Choir, singing in the finest concert halls in the United States and Europe, the experience that touched me the most was in Salt Lake City. The Sunday before Christmas, the Make-a-Wish Foundation brought a little girl to the Tabernacle to hear the Sunday broadcast. Afterward, she came up to the podium, and we sang a special arrangement of "Silent Night" for her. As she stood there with her mother's arms around her, I thought, *All the big events in the world don't compare for me to this one small focused moment.* I've heard my Primary songs sung at general conference, but I've also heard them at the American Fork Training School, sung by disabled children who could hardly learn or form words but had tears streaming down their faces while they sang.

I cherish beyond my ability to articulate it the sweet gospel experiences I have had through my involvement in music for the past twenty-plus years. And I can state unequivocally that it would never have happened without the continual and active support of my husband, Doug. He has encouraged me in every step along the way, provided financial support, helped me to achieve every musical goal, and often pushed me beyond my comfort zone to achieve something I thought impossible. He corrects and engraves all my hand-written music for publication, travels throughout the Church with me, setting up the sound equipment for firesides, speaks on the programs with me, and supports me in every aspect of my musical life.

Two years ago he felt a prompting that I should write one hundred hymns. I was incredulous. "One hundred hymns! I don't even know how! Hymns are not easy!" But now as I am finishing my seventy-first hymn (with texts mostly by Rodney Turner, John V. Pearson, David B. Larsen, Neal A. Maxwell, and Orrin G. Hatch), it has become one of the most enjoyable of all my musical endeavors and will, I hope, be an important part of the legacy I leave to my family and the Church.

Doug also encouraged me in the production of my own vocal album so my grandchildren and great-grandchildren could hear my voice and know me through my songs. That project was completed at the end of 1999. I honor him for the constancy of his love and support in helping me fulfill my dreams musically.

I am thankful to belong to a church that values music and understands its power. I especially love the simple music in our lives and worship. A few years ago a speaker at the Church Music Workshop, Minnie Hodapp, said, "I'm not in rebellion against the fine musicians, but as we admire orchids and roses, we also love sunflowers, asters and wayside offerings." I appreciate and respect great composers and their works and have been generously exposed to them through my years in BYU choruses, bands, and orchestras and in my years as a member of the Tabernacle Choir. Nevertheless, I offer my sincere voice in praise of simplicity and the idea that sometimes, in music, less can be more. President Kimball once said, "The message from and about Jesus Christ is so crucial to mankind that it was and is essential for that message to be kept exceedingly simple."

Elder Boyd K. Packer offers this strong statement: "Some of our most gifted people struggle to produce a work of art, hoping it will be described by the world as a masterpiece! Monumental! Epic! When in truth the simple 'I am a child of God' has moved and will move more souls to salvation than would such a work were they to succeed."[1]

The power of music seems to defy description. We know that the words, the melodies, and the rhythm combine to affect us profoundly, but how? We may never be able to answer that question satisfactorily, but perhaps Brigham Young told us all we need to know when he said, "The Lord, Himself, gave us the capacity to enjoy musical sounds."[2] Elder Packer adds: "We are able to feel and learn very quickly through music . . . some spiritual things that we would otherwise learn very slowly."[3]

I appreciate those who have paid the price in preparation and personal worthiness that they might be instruments in the Lord's hands in creating meaningful music for the Church and the world. Our goal as writers and composers should be to someday be able to say as Jesus once did, "Not I, but the Father that dwelleth within me—he doeth the works" (John 14:10). Elder Packer reminds us that "it is a mistake to assume that one can follow the ways of the world and then somehow in a moment of intruded inspiration, compose a great anthem of the Restoration. . . . When it is done, it will be done by one who has yearned and tried and longed fervently to do it." He further states that "inspiration can come to those whose talents are barely adequate and their contribution will be felt for generations."[4] That statement has given me great hope and encouragement through the years of my writing.

Inspiration is something I hesitate to talk about but treasure personally when it happens. When I received the assignment to write the Young Women values song I had difficulty seeing how to organize the seven values into a cohesive song. But after receiving assurances from the General Board that they were praying for me and then preparing myself spiritually, I had perhaps the most touching experience of any I have had while writing. I had the feeling that whoever else might have been asked to write "I Walk by Faith" would have written exactly the same song.

Where does our inspiration come from? President Hugh B. Brown said, "Sometimes during solitude I hear truth spoken with clarity and freshness . . . heard only with the soul, and I realize I brought it with me."

In the words of Elder Neal A. Maxwell: "When we rejoice in beautiful scenery, great art and great music, it is but the flexing of instincts acquired in another place and another time."[5]

I have had similar impressions during my writing. I felt moved upon by the Spirit one evening as I was writing alone and pondering the origin of my musical impulses, to write a song of gratitude to Him from whom our inspiration comes:

Thanks for the music that's in me.
Thanks for the warm and gentle magic of a melody.
Is it a memory that birth could not erase
Rising within me from another time and place?
Do I hear something that others do not hear?
Things that I sense I have heard before, but where?
Are these the sounds of heav'n that bring me to my knees
Saying thanks for the music in me?

I am so thankful for the music in me, in us, and so thankful that the Lord gave us the capacity to enjoy musical sounds. I will feel completely fulfilled in my writing endeavors if in a time of temptation some child should have come to his mind the words "I'm trying to be like Jesus"; or in times of teenage trials a young woman is comforted by the phrase "I walk by faith"; or if, in times of family contention, the words "love is spoken here" can help restore peace.

I echo the words of Newell Dayley to the Church Music Workshop in 1985: "It is worthy to desire musical excellence. We should do all in our power to increase our gifts that we might receive even more. We should hold to high standards. But, more importantly, we should be sensitive to the promptings of the Holy Spirit and do that which we are 'constrained' to do. Other musicians may see our most worthy efforts as *missing the mark*.

So be it. It's well for us to remember that which the prophet Jacob said about those who lived in Jerusalem: 'But behold [they] were a stiff-necked people; and they despised the words of plainness, . . . and sought for things that they could not understand. Wherefore, because of their blindness, which blindness came by *looking beyond the mark,* they must needs fall; for God hath taken away his plainness from them'."

I testify with all the sincerity of my heart that God's power can be felt in the plain and simple hymns and anthems of the Church. I feel that the musicians of the Church have a special mission and stewardship to cause this power to be manifest in the hearts of each member of the Church.

In that spirit I now share the stories behind one hundred of my gospel songs and include the lyrics for each one. Almost any words may be enhanced by a musical setting, but perhaps reading the words as poetry will give the reader more time for reflection and reveal my heart in a different way.

Notes

[1] Boyd K. Packer, *The Arts and the Spirit of the Lord,* BYU fireside address, Provo, Utah, 1 February 1976.

[2] Brigham Young, *Journal of Discourses,* 26 vols. (London: Latter-day Saints' Book Depot, 1854-86), 1:48.

[3] Packer, *Arts and the Spirit.*

[4] Packer, *Arts and the Spirit.*

[5] Neal A. Maxwell, *Ensign,* May 1984, 21.

-*Four*-

THE STORIES
BEHIND THE SONGS

I'll Follow Jesus

In 1976, at the age of thirty-eight, I decided to try writing gospel-oriented songs. "I'll Follow Jesus" was my first effort in that direction, and I see it as a defining moment in my life.

I had enjoyed the music that filled my childhood home, I had majored in music at Brigham Young University, and I had tried to teach my children to love good music. But I had been too busy rearing children, serving in the Church, and following my passion for playing on Church and city ball teams to think of writing music.

Now, however, the kids were all in school, and I had a few hours to call my own. While I was recovering from a serious sports injury the bishop asked me to write music for a roadshow. I loved doing it, and after the roadshow I tried writing popular songs—about twelve of them. That was fun but brought little fulfillment. Then I decided to add to the simple music of the Church that had meant so much to my own testimony. Our son Steve was a teenager and looking for music to sing as a solo in sacrament meeting. So, with time on my hands, an urging in my soul, and a reason to write (for Steve), I took that first step.

On a quiet afternoon when Doug had taken all the children somewhere for a few hours, I began. I prayed to know how and then took pencil and paper in hand and wrote words for the three verses and chorus of "I'll Follow Jesus." Then, experimenting at the piano, I wrote a simple accompaniment and put it down on music manuscript paper. I played and sang the song at least a dozen times—it was somehow a magical moment in which I think I first sensed the importance of what I was beginning.

When my family returned home I asked if they would like to hear my song. Doug, sensing it was very important to me, asked the children to sit quietly and listen. When I finished and turned to see their reaction, the tears in Doug's eyes were the encouragement I needed to continue writing.

I'll Follow Jesus
Words and music by Janice Kapp Perry

I'm only a child, I'm learning from day to day
I'm wondering how I'm going to find my way
Sometimes the path is clear and easy to see
Sometimes I feel a darker power calling me

Chorus
> I'll follow Jesus, I love His ways
> I want to be a child of His through all my days
> And though I slip and fall I'll rise again
> I'll follow Jesus and be true to Him

I'm trying to be a person that He would love
I'm trying to live so I will be worthy of
The gentle help He sends when we are in need
I want to follow in His footsteps where He leads

Repeat Chorus

I'm only a child, I'm searching the road ahead
I think of the things that Jesus has done and said
I know He'll guide me if I make Him my friend
So I will seek the loving Spirit He will send

Repeat Chorus

❖   ❖   ❖

A Young Boy Prayed

I have discovered through the years that ideas for songs do not always come at opportune times. I've also found that they usually come when I am alone and in a thoughtful frame of mind.

One day as I began a solo fifty-mile drive on the freeway between Provo and Salt Lake City, I began to think about the Joseph Smith story, which I had just read in the Pearl of Great Price. I felt absolute awe that a fourteen-year-old boy's humble prayer was answered with a heavenly vision that would change the course of mankind. I also realized that I had the same right as Joseph to kneel and pray to Heavenly Father and receive answers to my prayers. It was a very humbling and yet empowering thought.

Words and music just started happening in my mind. I reached for a scrap of paper in my purse and taped it to the center of the steering wheel. Each time a new line came I jotted it down (not a practice generally recommended for freeway driving!). When I reached my destination, I had three verses, a chorus, and the music in my mind and on a scrap of paper. I was afraid I wouldn't remember it later, so I sat in the car and drew staff lines on the back of a lube-and-oil invoice I found in the glove compartment and wrote out a rough version of the song before proceeding to my appointment.

This song was one of the first I wrote on gospel themes, and it was published and recorded just as it was conceived that day on I-15. In the recording studio the soloist, Brad Wilcox, was having a difficult time hitting one of the high notes in just the right way. After twenty minutes of frustration, vocal coach Randy Boothe stopped the session and had us all gather together while he offered a prayer for help from the Lord. The soloist returned to the microphone and sang the phrase perfectly on the next try. Our needs may be smaller than Joseph's but the Lord does hear and answer each prayer of faith.

A Young Boy Prayed
Words and music by Janice Kapp Perry

As a child I learned at my mother's knee
What a prayer of faith to a child can be
As she told of a boy with a troubled mind
Whose prayer was answered for all mankind

Chorus
> A young boy prayed
> And opened up the heavens with his faith
> Because he prayed
> He heard and saw the Father face to face
> This simple truth helps me in all I do
> Because I know that I can pray too

How I love to hear of the sacred place
Where he talked with Jesus and saw His face
When I'm all alone and I kneel in prayer
I close my eyes and pretend I'm there

Repeat Chorus

As I go through life with its good and bad
I will try to think of the faith he had
I can pray to the Father to comfort me
As Joseph did in that grove of trees

Repeat Chorus

❖   ❖   ❖

In the Hollow of Thy Hand

In 1977 my good friend Monita Robison came to me with a request. Her son Scott was soon to leave on a mission, and she had written lyrics for a song entitled "In the Hollow of Thy Hand" and wondered if I would compose the music. I had read that phrase in the scriptures and thought it a very comforting idea that the Lord would hold someone safe in "the hollow of His hand." Our oldest son's mission was also imminent, so my feelings matched Monita's exactly.

Parents throughout the Church share these same tender feelings as their sons and daughters leave their homes for missionary service—perhaps that accounts for the rapid spread of this song throughout the Church following its publication. It was an amazing and unexpected phenomenon. Over the years we have received scores of thank-you letters for providing a song that expresses parents' feelings as their children leave on missions; ten different writers have sent copies of their choral arrangements of the song; at least ten parents have sent their adaptation of the words for their daughter's farewell; several families have sent adaptations of the words to fit a funeral for a family member; and many have orchestrated it or added instruments. The outpouring of interest and emotion over the song truly testify of the tender emotions of the Saints as their children leave the safety of their homes to bring souls to Christ and to sanctify themselves.

After twenty-plus years I received a call from a very honest person who said, "Have you written anything else for missionaries? I have heard this song at so many farewells I am sick of it!" When I chuckled, she added, "Oh, I didn't mean that the way it sounded—it's a great song. It's just that it's all I've heard for so many years!" I considered that a compliment.

In the Hollow of Thy Hand

Words by Monita Turley Robison
Music by Janice Kapp Perry

Dear Lord, who blesses us with love,
Please send this day Thy Spirit from above
As this Thy son accepts a call from Thee
Help him, we pray, to learn humility
Direct his footsteps every day
And keep him ever walking in Thy ways
Inspire him as he spreads the gospel plan
Lord, hold him in the hollow of Thy hand

Chorus
   In the hollow of Thy hand
   As he grows from boy to man
   Help his understanding deepen and increase
   In the hollow of Thy hand
   As he grows from boy to man
   Let him know the special blessing of Thy peace

Dear Lord, who hears and answers prayers,
Please keep Thy servant always in Thy care
As he prepares to teach his fellowmen
Oh, keep him safe and bring him home again
Protect him from all worldly ways

And always send Thy Spirit when he prays
Give him the courage of a righteous man
Just hold him in the hollow of Thy hand

Repeat Chorus

   In the hollow of Thy hand
   As he grows from boy to man
   Help his understanding deepen and increase
   As he faces life's demands
   May he take a valiant stand
   Give him shelter in the hollow of Thy hand

❖   ❖   ❖

Where Is Heaven?

I wrote "Where Is Heaven?" on a melancholy afternoon when I was thinking about our little son Richard, who had lived for just a few hours following his birth. I often found myself wondering exactly where he was and what he was doing during this time of our separation from him. I strained to remember our premortal existence, hoping to find comfort from recalling what had happened there. But the veil remained firmly in place, and I knew I had to walk by faith for now. My comfort came from realizing that the only glimpse of heaven I can have right now is that which I feel in the presence of my earthly family. I prayed that Richie felt that same happiness with those we love who are on the other side of the veil.

Where Is Heaven?
Words and music by Janice Kapp Perry

I wish I could remember the days before my birth
And if I knew the Father before I came to earth
In quiet moments when I'm all alone
I close my eyes and try to see my heav'nly home

Chorus
   Where is heaven?
   Is it very far?

I would like to know if it's
Beyond the brightest star.
Where is heaven?
Will you show the way?
I would like to learn and grow
And go there some day

I wish I could remember the Father's loving face
And all the friends and family that filled that holy place
Was I a child there? Did I walk with God?
And was that where I learned about the Iron Rod?

Repeat Chorus

Although I can't remember and cannot clearly see
I listen to the Spirit, and so I must believe
But still I wonder, and I hope to find
The answer to the question that is on my mind

Repeat Chorus

I've a feeling that it's not so far
When you're with the ones you love
It's right where you are

❖   ❖   ❖

Imagine Me, a Missionary

It is never too early to plant the idea of being a missionary in the hearts of our little children. In 1978, my cousin Joy Saunders Lundberg wrote and illustrated a delightful children's book on that subject, entitled *Me, a Missionary*. I was especially pleased when she asked me to write a song for the book that would help children remember the concept.

As I wrote the song I imagined how a young child might feel day-dreaming in his bedroom about where he might someday be called on a mission. I made it upbeat, happy, and memorable as I listed many countries he might be called to.

Joy and I later collaborated on the musical *It's a Miracle*, which toured the United States for three years. This little piece became an important part of the family scene in which the mother is trying to help her son feel excited about serving someday as a full-time missionary. Hearing it performed in 239 shows seems to have had the desired effect on the children in our cast: almost all of them later served missions. We hope it had that effect on the thousands of others who saw the show, for our purpose was to promote missionary service.

Imagine Me, a Missionary
Words and music by Janice Kapp Perry

When it's time for my mission
I may be sent to Hong Kong
Or to Mexico City or to Germany or Spain
I could love any country
If that's where the Lord should want me
Though the language is diff'rent
The message is the same

Chorus
    Imagine me, a missionary trav'ling through the land
    Imagine me, a missionary doin' what I can
    To spread the gospel message in the latter day
    I must study and learn and listen
    And prepare in ev'ry way

Oh, I may take my message
To the Indian Nation
Or to old Argentina or to Russia or Brazil
I don't care where they send me
For the people will befriend me
And then that is the mission
I'll love the best of all

Repeat Chorus

❖ ❖ ❖

A Missionary's Prayer

After the early death of my father, Jacob Kapp, at fifty-seven years of age, my mother, Ruth, filled her life with many positive things. She crocheted, she quilted, she played in a dance band, and she accompanied the Senior Citizen Fun Band. She wrote several volumes of her life history and researched and entered more than forty thousand names for temple work. Her happy, productive life, centered around her children and grandchildren, was very fulfilling to her. Nevertheless, in her late sixties she began to feel the prompting to leave her secure, peaceful life for full-time missionary service. Throughout her life she had been a dedicated missionary, bringing many into the Church during her service as a stake missionary. She and Dad had hoped to serve a full-time mission, but now she gathered her courage to go alone.

At age sixty-nine, Mother was called to the Louisiana Baton Rouge Mission, which was later realigned as the Mississippi Jackson Mission. As her children, we had a few misgivings about sending our mother out into the world alone, but we knew well the extraordinary Nephi-like faith she had to "go and do the things which the Lord hath commanded," knowing he would "prepare a way" (1 Nephi 3:7).

The words for "A Missionary's Prayer" were written especially for my mother. The first phrase—"Father, I hear thy call, I turn my thoughts to thee, forsaking all"—described exactly her attitude about leaving. Our son Steve performed the song at her farewell and also at his own farewell four months later when he left for the Belgium Antwerp Mission.

Mother was a marvelous missionary, bringing many to the waters of baptism. She was at first paired with older sister missionaries, but the president soon realized that her high energy and enthusiasm would be put to better use as a trainer for the young sister missionaries. She walked about five miles a day, carrying books and teaching aids for most of her mission. Only toward the end of her mission, when the president was shocked to learn she was seventy, did she receive a car to drive.

A Missionary's Prayer

Words and music by Janice Kapp Perry

Father, I hear thy call
I turn my thoughts to Thee, forsaking all
Recalling promises we all must keep
I put my hand in Thine and go to feed Thy sheep

Lead me to those who seek
And give me faith and strength to boldly speak
In humble dignity I will proclaim
That men may come to know and love Thy holy name

Chorus
    If there be trials, Lord, to help me grow
    If Thou wilt guide me I will conquer this I know
    I will go and do the things which the Lord commandeth
    For I know that He giveth no commands to His children
    Except He prepare a way
    Except He prepare a way

Father, I clearly see
That ev'ry lasting joy has come from Thee
Help me to serve Thee well and thus repay
Thy loving kindness I receive from day to day

Knowing that Thou art near
And I may seek Thy help through daily prayer
I'll walk in confidence that I will see
Thy spirit touch the lives of seeking men through me

Repeat Chorus

❖   ❖   ❖

My Star Is Rising

About a year after I began writing gospel music in earnest, our stake Young Women president asked if I would write a theme song for their approaching Young Women conference. They had chosen the theme "My Star Is Rising," and the Laurel presidents from the eight wards in our stake were to form a chorus to introduce the theme song to the girls after which all the girls in the stake would sing it.

I loved their theme and went to work enthusiastically. Although I had been a tomboy in my younger years, I had always felt very comfortable and happy with my being a woman and decided to begin the song with a strong affirmation of that fact: "May the light of my womanhood shine bright and crystal clear through all time." I knew the young girls in our ward well and could see they were approaching the time when they would be making major life decisions. I hoped my song would help them feel confidence in themselves and their womanhood in this critical time.

Hearing the song performed at the conference was very rewarding to me, as it was a new experience to hear the notes and words I had written come to life. I later came to think of the song in a completely different sense when it was performed at the baptism of Tina Gunn, BYU's six-foot, five-inch basketball star, before her marriage to Scott Robison of our ward. She was already a bonafide star on her team, but at her baptism her star was rising in a totally new way.

My Star Is Rising
Words and music by Janice Kapp Perry

May the light of my womanhood
Shine bright and crystal clear through all time
As the torchlight is passed to me
I'll hold it high, hold it high
This is the time, oh yes, these are the golden years
And I will meet the test somehow
Oh, I can see I'm coming to an open door
I feel it now

Chorus
    My star is rising
    And I feel a gentle surge
    As new horizons come into view
    I see before me many roads to take
    What should I say?
    What should I do?
    My star is rising

May the light of my womanhood
Shine bright with purity from now on
Though the world tries to conquer me
I'll travel on, travel on
For I am reaching upward to my destiny
And I can see the golden sky
I know I'm making mem'ries for eternity
The world is mine

Repeat Chorus

It's rising
Today my star is rising

❖   ❖   ❖

I'm Trying to Be like Jesus

Local Church leaders who were planning a regional Primary conference asked me to write a song for the conference. The theme was kindness, and "I'm Trying to Be like Jesus" was the result. As I pondered and prayed about that subject I felt sure the best way to approach it was to plant the idea in the children's hearts of trying to become like the kindest man who ever lived, our Savior Jesus Christ. Every aspect of His life reflected kindness and caring, even to the point of forgiving those who were crucifying Him.

Michael F. Moody, chairman of the Church Music Committee, became an advocate of the song, which he said contained "the essence of the gospel." It was published in the *Ensign* and eventually in the *Children's Songbook*.

A few years after publishing the song I was invited to the American Fork Training School to attend seminary graduation where a chorus of handicapped students would be performing several of my songs. I arrived early and was already seated as approximately twenty young adults filed into the room, each one giving me a hug and saying a heartfelt "I love you!" My feelings were very tender long before they began singing and

I truly felt humbled in their presence. If only the whole world could express love as freely and naturally as they did.

The concert was moving! As they sang the finale, "I'm Trying to Be like Jesus," I felt like shouting "You are, you are like Jesus!" One young man in the front row with Down syndrome was unable to learn the words but sang "sounds" from his heart that caused tears to roll down his cheeks. My heart nearly broke at the sweetness of the moment!

I left there with a taped recording of the singing and replayed it while doing dishes that evening. An unknowing family member said, "What is that awful sound?" I was completely shocked and could only say, "This is one time when you truly had to be there."

I'm Trying to Be like Jesus
Words and music by Janice Kapp Perry

I'm trying to be like Jesus
I'm following in His ways
I'm trying to love as He did
In all that I do and say
At times I am tempted
To make a wrong choice
But I try to listen
As the still small voice whispers

Chorus
 Love one another as Jesus loves you
 Try to show kindness in all that you do
 Be gentle and loving in deed and in thought
 For these are the things Jesus taught

I'm trying to love my neighbor
I'm learning to serve my friends
I watch for the day of gladness
When Jesus will come again
I try to remember
The lessons He taught
Then the Holy Spirit
Enters into my thoughts, saying

Repeat Chorus

Love Is Spoken Here

Sometimes ideas for songs come at unusual times and in unusual places. "Love Is Spoken Here" definitely had an unusual beginning. My husband and I were attending a party in honor of an outgoing stake presidency, and during a lull in the activities I said to him, "Please help me come up with an interesting idea for a song. I want to enter the *Ensign* Songwriting Contest, and the deadline is just two days away."

"How long have you known about this?" he asked.

"Well, just this one . . . year," I admitted. He rolled his eyes but said he would try.

As we were leaving our host's home that evening, Doug pointed to a beautiful cross-stitched sampler above the kitchen sink. It read "Love Is Spoken Here." "There's your title," he said. "Go to it."

I loved the idea! I tried to discover who had coined the phrase but could not. The thought reminded me of the home I had grown up in, and I decided to write about two things that gave me a feeling of peace and security in that home—hearing my mother's prayers and feeling the power of my father's priesthood. I wrote one verse about each of them which could be sung at the same time over a common harmonic structure. This was my first experiment with counter melodies.

The piece did well in the contest and was published in the *Ensign*. A few years later a Primary teacher from Texas wrote to say, "We've enjoyed learning your song 'Love Is Spoken Here' and are writing to ask permission to make the phrase into a cross-stitch sampler." That seemed only right. The phrase had come full circle from a cross-stitch sampler, to my song, to the *Ensign,* to a Primary in Texas, and back to a cross-stitch sampler.

I've had countless sweet experiences with this song, including a performance by the Tabernacle Choir during my term in the choir. Another experience that touched me deeply occurred during a presentation at a stake women's conference in Provo, Utah. I asked for a volunteer to sing one of the melodies while I sang the other. The hand of a teenaged girl with Down syndrome shot up immediately, and I invited her to join me. *If she can't do it,* I thought, *I'll just sing along with her.* "Which part would you like to sing?" I asked.

"Either," she replied with complete confidence and to the delight of the audience.

I assigned her the first part, started the taped accompaniment, and stood in awe as Amy Monson performed one of the sweetest renditions of that song I will ever hear. When it was my turn, I could hardly sing through the lump in my throat and almost had to ask for *her* help. When we sang our parts together, she held up her end perfectly, gave me a hug, and returned to her seat. The audience couldn't restrain themselves from applauding her through their tears.

On one occasion the words of this song came back to haunt me. We had been tending our three little granddaughters who were four, three, and one for eleven days while their parents enjoyed a trip to Europe. They were sweet little girls, but I was not used to such a routine and grew more and more tired each day. On the evening before their parents returned I tucked the two older girls into bed, saying, "Grandma is *very* tired—I need you to go right to sleep while I get the baby to bed." As I was giving the baby her bottle, I heard everything break loose in the older girls' room—pillow fighting, jumping on the bed, and giggling. I was determined to get the baby to sleep before I went in there, but my feelings were rising during this time. Finally, I marched in to confront the older girls, saying very firmly, "Jessie and Rachel, I want you to lie down and pull the covers up to your chin. I am going to *watch* you go to sleep!" Never having heard this tone of voice from their grandmother, they dived under the covers and didn't move. Then I heard a tiny voice say in the dimly lit room, "Grandma, will you sing one of your Primary songs for us?" I was in no mood, but finally said in my same firm voice, "All right. I'll sing *one* song, but *only* one— don't ask for two. Which one do you want?" After a slight hesitation, the tiny voice whispered, "'Love Is Spoken Here.'" Feeling like the worst hypocrite who had ever written a song, I repented quickly, sang the song, and watched them go to sleep.

Love Is Spoken Here

Words and music by Janice Kapp Perry

First Verse

 I see my mother kneeling
 With our family each day
 I hear the words she whispers
 As she bows her head to pray
 Her plea to the Father
 Quiets all my fears
 And I am thankful
 Love is spoken here

Second Verse

 Mine is a home where every hour
 Is blessed by the strength of priesthood pow'r
 With father and mother leading the way
 Teaching me how to trust and obey
 And the things they teach are crystal clear
 For love is spoken here

Both Verses Together

I can often feel the Savior near
When love is spoken here

❖ ❖ ❖

Well Done, Thou Good and Faithful Servant

Every faithful follower of Jesus Christ looks forward to the time when he has successfully completed his life's journey and returns worthily to the embrace of the Savior to hear the words, "Well done, thou good and faithful servant." Just the anticipation of experiencing that moment of utter spiritual ecstacy can help us avoid many temptations that might set us on a path leading to some other, much less satisfying conclusion. Often when I see young missionaries return from faithful service in their mission, on fire with the spirit of the gospel, I have a strong impression that the Lord is pleased with their offering and would speak "well done" to their souls. This piece was written for such an occasion as my cousin Cory Saunders returned from his mission.

A few years later, while I spent time with another cousin, Shirley Ross Catron, during the last months of her life, I modified the words so they would be appropriate for her funeral service. Her faith had remained strong through very difficult circumstances, and I had no doubt she would be hearing these words personally from the Savior very soon. Her last request of me was to help her obtain a current temple recommend before she died, as hers had expired during her illness. Her bishop was happy to meet this request.

My own mother outlined her own funeral service long before she died—and even recorded her own organ prelude music! At the bottom of her instructions we read: "I would like to have someone sing Jani's song 'Well Done, Thou Good and Faithful Servant' at my funeral service, but *only if you feel I have truly earned it!*" It was sung by her grandson, Steven Kapp Perry.

Both the missionary version and funeral adaptation are included here.

Well Done, Thou Good and Faithful Servant
Words and music by Janice Kapp Perry

You were called to serve a mission
By a prophet of the Lord
And you've borne your solemn witness
That the gospel was restored
You were called that you might testify
And teach your fellow man
The simple truths of Jesus
In an unfamiliar land

Yes, each child of God
Has promises to keep
For the Savior has said
"If ye love me, feed my sheep"

Chorus
> Well done, thou good and faithful servant
> Well done, thou good and faithful one

You have seen the field is white
You have shared the gospel light
You have earned the Savior's gentle praise
"Well done"

You were called to help your brother
Find the straight and narrow way
As the Savior's true disciple
You were led by Him each day
In the service of your fellowman
You're only serving God
Fulfilling His commission
That all men must be taught

In man-measured time
Your mission now is done
But a lifetime of joy serving others
Has just begun

Repeat Chorus

Well done

Well Done, Thou Good and Faithful Servant (funeral benediction)
Words and music by Janice Kapp Perry

You were nurtured by the Father
In the days before your birth
Choosing there the plan of Jesus
To be tested here on earth
With a veil upon your memory
You've lived by faith alone
In keeping His commandments
Your love and faith have grown

For each child of God
Must walk the narrow way
And His light shining brightly
Has led you from day to day

Chorus
Well done, thou good and faithful servant
Well done, thou good and faithful one
You have known the gospel light

You have fought a winning fight
You have earned the Savior's gentle praise
"Well done"

You have led your faithful loved ones
   (*alt:* You have walked with faithful loved ones)
In the straight and narrow way
As the Savior's true disciple
You were led by Him each day
Giving service to your fellowman
Reflected love of God
And all that you have given
Now turns to your reward

In man-measured time
Your mission now is done
But eternity's joy in His Kingdom
Has just begun

Repeat Chorus

Well done

❖   ❖   ❖

The Field Is White

In 1981 our son Robert was called to serve in the Seoul Korea Mission. I looked on our world globe to find that country which I had mostly associated with news reports from the Korean War. I felt very grateful that he was being sent there to teach the gospel of peace rather than to participate in a war and hoped with all my heart that he would find some who would be willing to embrace the gospel message.

While I was pondering what music I might write for his mission farewell, I noticed subtle changes taking place in his bedroom. On his nightstand I noticed a set of scriptures and a small Korean hymnbook. Above his bed was a newly posted painting of Christ by his uncle Gary Kapp. I looked at the ski poster on his wall—a dramatic scene with a skier cutting through a vast white slope of new snow, powder flying. Robb loved to ski, and I knew that was one sacrifice he was making to serve a mission.

The idea for his song was born in that moment as I looked at the pristine field of white snow and recalled the scripture in Doctrine and Covenants 6:3—"Behold, the field is white already to harvest; therefore, whoso desireth to reap, let him thrust in his sickle with his might, and reap while the day lasts, that he may treasure up for his soul everlasting salvation in the kingdom of God."

I felt so pleased at Robb's willingness to give up one field of white for another that was of far-reaching and eternal significance. I called the song "The Field Is White."

The Field Is White
Words and music by Janice Kapp Perry

Joseph sought the Lord while in his youth
Desiring in his heart to know the truth
As he knelt alone to ask of God
Divinely, simply he was taught
He was a boy, loved of the Father
Called to restore to earth the gospel plan
He was a boy with seeds of godhood growing deep within
Led by the Spirit, he taught his fellowman

The field was white
The harvest lay before him
The time was right
For men to hear God's word
The field was white
And he who labored served with all his might
In the harvest season of the Lord

Father, here before us is a youth
Desiring in his heart to teach the truth
As he leaves his home for distant lands
Please guide him with Thy loving hands
He is a boy, called by a prophet
Willing to serve and teach his fellowman
He is a boy with seeds of godhood growing deep within
Led by the Spirit, he'll teach the gospel plan

The field is white
The harvest lies before him
The time is right
For men to hear God's word
The field is white
O ye that labor, serve with all your might
In the harvest season of the Lord

The field is white
The field is white

❖   ❖   ❖

The Things of Eternity

One day in 1981 I asked my mother if she had any good ideas for a song title. I wanted to write but needed a focus. She said, "Write one called 'The Things of Eternity'." I liked the idea but got sidetracked and didn't get to it. Two years later, I asked her again for a good song title, and she said, "I gave you my best one two years ago, and you didn't do it. I can't give you another one until that one is done."

This time I got right to it. I first interviewed *her* about what "the things of eternity" meant to her. Then I added some of my own ideas. I can't remember which were her ideas and which were mine, but I do remember that we loved talking about it together. She had definitely lived a life that was focused on the things of eternity, and as I wrote the song I committed once more in my heart to follow her great example.

The Things of Eternity
Words and music by Janice Kapp Perry

When I feel love in my home
Or faith that has grown
Or kneel with a loved one humbly praying
When friendships are strong
When strangers belong
The Spirit stirs within me, saying:

Chorus
These are the things of eternity
These are the things that are sure
They light the path for the journey home
Where good things will endure

When I have faith in the Lord
And live by His word
In sickness I ask in faith for healing
And when priesthood pow'r
Is felt in that hour
My heart is filled with one sweet feeling

Repeat Chorus

And when the light in my eye
Shows pure love of Christ
And when gospel truth and light surround me
When love tears are wept
When covenants are kept
I feel God's love in all around me

Repeat Chorus

And I pray my heart will ever be
On the things of eternity

❖   ❖   ❖

I Love to See the Temple

Not long after I began writing children's songs, a stake Primary president in our area instituted a weekly five-minute temple presentation in the wards in her stake. She requested that I write a theme song the children could sing each week to remind them it was time for the temple presentation. I loved the assignment and began reviewing some of my early feelings about the temple.

As a teenager growing up on a farm in Oregon, I rarely saw a temple but occasionally traveled with my youth group to the Idaho Falls Temple to perform baptisms for the dead. Each time we rounded the curve into that city and caught our first view of the temple, these words passed silently through my mind: "I love to see the temple!" I chose that simple, heartfelt phrase as the title for my new temple song.

Beginning with our marriage in the Logan Utah Temple, my husband and I have attended many temples throughout the world. I still love to see the temple, but I especially enjoy *being inside* that "place of love and beauty" and participating in the holy ordinances that are performed there.

Today, I can see the Provo Temple from the window of my home and love to hear my grandchildren sing "I Love to See the Temple" when they come for a visit. My morning walking path circles around the temple grounds, and as I pass by I feel a deep gratitude that our little son Richard, who only lived on earth for a few hours, can be ours forever because of the sealing ordinances of the temple.

We recently met a young couple from the Midwest who had earlier traveled to the Washington Temple to attend sessions. Each parent planned to take a turn tending their young daughter on the temple grounds while the other attended a session. The mother had sung her little daughter to sleep with the song "I Love to See the Temple" and then proceeded to her session. Sadly, the child suffered a fatal accident on the temple grounds during the session. Her mother said it brought her a measure of comfort to know the words of that song were the last words her little daughter had heard from her.

I Love to See the Temple

Words and music by Janice Kapp Perry

I love to see the temple
I'm going there someday
To feel the Holy Spirit
To listen and to pray
For the temple is a house of God
A place of love and beauty
I'll prepare myself
While I am young
This is my sacred duty

I love to see the temple
I'll go inside some day
I'll cov'nant with my Father
I'll promise to obey
For the temple is a holy place
Where we are sealed together
As a child of God
I've learned this truth
"A fam'ly is forever"

(The following verse was later added for the SATB arrangement.)

I love to see the temple
Shine brightly through the night
A beacon to all people
Of purity and light
For the temple is a sacred place
Where worthy Saints assemble
To receive the holy ord'nances
Performed in God's own temple

   This holy house brings peace to me
   I love to see
   I love to see the temple

❖   ❖   ❖

He Will Make Mighty His Sons

After the death of Richie, our fifth child, in 1968 from Rh-factor complications, our doctor said we would not be able to have more children. We had hoped for a larger family, so we began opening our home to foster children—not through an agency (except for a Navajo son we had for eight years) but just to whomever had a need. In the end we had fifteen different boys and one girl stay with us anywhere from a few weeks to five years' time.

One of our foster sons was brought to our home by his father, who wanted him to be safe from the serious abuse of his moth-er—just for two weeks.

We had first met Tim (not his real name) when he was in the hospital with broken legs, having been run over by his mother's car. Now this sixteen-year-old came to us tied in knots, emotionally and physically, and brought nothing with him. When he removed his shirt to put on one of our son's T-shirts for bed, we saw scars from iron burns on his shoulder. When his shoes and socks came off, we saw scars from knife cuts on his feet. Telling his story would fill a whole volume by itself and is not possible in this context.

Tim lived with us for over a year. He had a genius I.Q., and merely from being in a peaceful place he progressed from flunking all his classes to getting straight A's, thereby earning a scholarship to BYU based only on his senior year. His abrasive voice and manner softened, he learned to give and receive love, and he began to recover gradually from his deep emotional scars.

Nevertheless, he waged a constant battle against low self-esteem, and when it was time for a mission he expressed doubts that he could be a successful missionary. Words didn't help much, so I turned to music to try to help him see the vision of what he could accomplish with the Lord's help. I spoke of Joseph, Helaman's warriors, David, and Mormon, who were young men "made strong by the power of God's grace."

Tim felt the message of the song, which was sung at his farewell. He served an honorable mission to Sweden and still valiantly struggles to overcome the effects of his early and constant abuse.

He Will Make Mighty His Sons
Words and music by Janice Kapp Perry

Often the Lord, when a work must be done
Will accomplish His purposes through those who are young
Armed with faith and with truth, and the strength of their youth
They work miracles, reach pinnacles, and great things are wrought
For they're filled with the Spirit of God

If Joseph, at fourteen, could call down a vision
With simple, unwavering faith
If David in his youth could stand with Goliath
Made strong by the pow'r of God's grace

If He could make mighty all these
I know He will also bless me

Now, as before, there's a work to be done
And the Lord's chosen messengers are those who are young
Ev'ry worthy one called, by a prophet of God
To declare the word, and serve the Lord, and great things are wrought
For they're filled with the Spirit of God

If Helaman's warriors were strong in their boy years
Because they were righteously taught
If Mormon, a young boy, commanded an army
That marched in the power of God
If He could make mighty all these
I know He will also bless me

Bridge
>   If He saw their desires and sent heaven's fire
>   To cleanse them and light their way
>   If He gave them His grace and showed them His face
>   Will He not do the same today
>   If He could make mighty all these
>   I know He will also bless me

Though alone I am weak, His blessing I'll seek
Then whatever my mission may be
I am ready, dear Father, send me
I am ready, dear Father, send me

❖   ❖   ❖

Lord, Are You There?

It was extremely frustrating to lose the use of my left hand
for playing the piano just as I began writing music. I couldn't
believe it was happening, but I felt very sure that if I just mus-
tered enough faith the Lord would take away this affliction.
After all, I was devoting my time to writing music that would
praise and honor Him, so it seemed only fair.

Medical tests produced no diagnosis or cure. Priesthood
blessings alluded to a time in the future when the healing

might come. My frustration led me to read about the lives of such men as Paul and Job, whose thorns in the flesh were not removed despite their worthiness. I also became more aware of people around me whose physical problems were much greater than mine. They seemed worthy of a healing blessing, and yet for reasons known only to the Lord, the blessing was withheld.

I have always believed that every heartfelt prayer is heard and answered by the Lord. I have never wavered in that belief, so through this time of soul searching I gradually acknowledged that the Lord was indeed hearing my prayers, feeling my anguish, and even responding to my prayer—but for now the answer was no.

My spirit matured immensely through this experience, as I progressed from pleading "Lord, are you there? Do you hear my prayer?" to eventually receiving an assurance that He is there, I have been heard, and He is answering in a way He knows is best for me.

Lord, Are You There?
Words and music by Janice Kapp Perry

Female First Part
> Lord, are you there? Do you hear my prayer?
> Sometimes it is hard to know
> Yet here, as I kneel, my heart seems to feel
> A warm and comforting glow

Male First Part
> Child, you must believe
> Just ask and you shall receive
> Knock, knock, I'll open the door
> I cannot promise you more

Female and Male First Parts Together

Female
> Lord, I have read and believed in Thy word
> "If any lack wisdom, let him ask of God."
> With a heart that is broken, the words have been spoken
> Please let me know I am heard

Female Second Part
> Lord, are you there? Do you really care?
> I listen but cannot hear
> Sometimes when I call my voice seems so small
> I wonder, Lord, can you hear

Male Second Part
> Child, I love you so
> But sometimes the answer is no
> Pray, pray, I'll open the way
> And this is how you will grow

Female and Male Second Parts Together

Male
> Child, you have read and believed in my word
> "If any lack wisdom, let him ask of God."
> With a heart that is broken the words have been spoken
> A loving Father has heard

Female	*Male*
Lord, are you there?	Child, you must believe
Do you hear my prayer?	Just ask and you shall receive

❖   ❖   ❖

Mother, Tell Me the Story

I thought it would be nice to include a lullaby when we were preparing to record our first album of children's songs. I enjoy the idea of having two different melodies sung separately and then at the same time, and thought this would be a natural format for a mother-child exchange at bedtime. My favorite childhood bedtime memories are of my mother lying beside me on my bed telling faith-promoting stories and assuring me of her love. Peaceful sleep always followed such sweet moments.

When "Mother, Tell Me the Story" was published in the *Children's Songbook*, I was asked to write an optional verse that spoke of Jesus' nearness and His watching over us as we sleep. I include both verses here.

Mother, Tell Me the Story

Words and music by Janice Kapp Perry

Child

> Mother, tell me the story
> That I love to hear
> Tell me of heaven
> And why I came here
> Mother, tell how you love me
> And gently speak
> And then I'll go to sleep

Mother

> Child, I am here
> Can you feel that heaven is near?
> Sleep, sleep; a lovewatch I'll keep
> To protect you through the night

Both Parts Together

(Optional Verse)

Child

> Mother*, tell me of Jesus
> And how He is near
> Tell how He loves me
> And I will not fear
> Mother, tell how His Spirit
> Brings comfort and peace
> And then I'll go to sleep

Mother (or Father)

> Child, He is there
> In His love you never need fear
> Sleep, sleep; a lovewatch He'll keep
> To protect you through the night

alternate word: Daddy

❖   ❖   ❖

Thanks for the Music

Music constantly plays in my mind. It is not always in my conscious mind, but at any time of the day (and often at night) when I take the time to notice, there is some kind of melody or rhythm going on in the background of my thoughts. Some are familiar songs; others are made-up sequences that just entertain me or occupy my subconscious for a time.

Often when Doug is holding my hand, he'll ask, "What are you playing?" Until he speaks I have not been aware that I am playing *anything,* but he feels it in my fingers, and when he asks, I can identify it and hum the tune for him. When I write music through the evening, that music generally continues to play in my mind all through the night as I sleep fitfully. After Tabernacle Choir rehearsals, one of the songs we have practiced invariably keeps me company all through the night. I have often wondered if this phenomenon is a blessing or a curse!

In more introspective moments, I wonder whether the music I hear is "rising within me from another time and place" and whether I hear some things that others do not hear. Every person is given a gift, and I feel certain that mine is related to music.

One evening in 1983 I felt an overwhelming gratitude for whatever gift of music is in me. I first knelt to express my feelings to Heavenly Father and then felt a strong desire to express these feelings musically.

"Thanks for the Music" is a song of gratitude to Heavenly Father for the music that touches and influences my life—both others' music and my own. I am deeply grateful for music that comforts me, inspires me, helps me to worship more meaningfully, fills my lonely hours, and enhances my joy even in the happiest times. I am especially grateful when music I have conceived and written is meaningful to others in the different circumstances of their lives.

Thanks for the Music
Words and music by Janice Kapp Perry

Chorus
> Thanks for the music that's in me
> Thanks for the warm and gentle magic of a melody
> Is it a mem'ry that birth could not erase
> Rising within me from another time and place?
> Do I hear something that others do not hear?
> Things that I sense I have heard before, but where?
> Are these the sounds of heav'n that bring me to my knees?
> Saying thanks for the music in me

In the quiet times, when I'm all alone
I close my eyes and think about the melodies I've known
In the lonely hours, sitting silently
The songs that make me whole again keep coming back to me

Repeat Chorus

In the rev'rent hours when I know He's there
I raise my voice to heaven and my song becomes a prayer
And when life is good, and my heart is full
Sweet music deep within me stirs to fill my mind and soul

Repeat Chorus

Thanks for the music

❖   ❖   ❖

This Life Is Just the Beginning

In 1982 my cousins asked if I would write a song for their parents' thirty-fifth wedding anniversary. This couple, Merv and Rae Preston, were well-loved and respected in our extended family, and I felt pleased to honor them in this way.

They had worked as hard throughout their lives as anyone else I had ever known, but their hard work never seemed to translate into financial security, and they faced frequent challenges in that area. Their service in the Church was exemplary—helping others seemed to be the goal and mission of their lives.

In spite of temporal struggles, their personal relationship as a couple was a fascinating love story that touched and entertained family members through the years. Good-natured teasing and constant comical declarations of love brought smiles to all of us. In writing their song I could envision eternal happiness for them just being more of the same relationship they have enjoyed here on earth.

They are now well past their fiftieth anniversary, and they just keep on keeping on in the same admirable way. I have no doubt this love story will go on forever—though minus the wheelchair and the pain someday.

This Life Is Just the Beginning
Words and music by Janice Kapp Perry

Looking back through the years
Through the laughter, though the tears
I just recall a life full of caring
Thinking back for a while
Through the struggles, through the smiles
Life has been good because we were sharing

Chorus
>   This life is just the beginning
>   Somehow I know there's more
>   This life is but a moment
>   Then comes the time we're living for
>   They say eternity is filled with love
>   And if it's really true
>   Then eternity will just be more of you

Looking back through our days
I recall your loving ways
I have known joy when we were together
I have loved you alone
And I guess I've always known
Our kind of love will go on forever

Repeat Chorus

❖   ❖   ❖

We'll Bring the World His Truth

"We'll Bring the World His Truth," which Primary children throughout the Church often refer to as "The Helaman Song," was written in response to a request from a stake Primary chorister in north Provo. She was leading a two hundred-voice children's chorus for a stake conference in the Marriott Center at BYU. The theme for the meeting was missionary work, and she asked that I write a stirring song that would help children realize their missionary responsibility.

I knew that most of the children in the choir were from strong LDS families, so they had been taught gospel principles from an early age. In many ways they truly were "as the army of Helaman"—they had heard and believed the testimony of "goodly parents," prophets, and teachers and would have a responsibility throughout their lives to share that message.

Beginning with that first performance, I have always delighted to hear the great enthusiasm with which the children sing the chorus. I was sitting on the stand a few years later in Birmingham, Alabama, when a large Primary chorus standing directly behind me shouted it out with such amazing force it startled me and greatly amused the audience!

A musical highlight of my life happened in January 1999 after my husband and I had finished speaking at the Missionary Training Center devotional. Twenty-two hundred elders and sisters rose and powerfully sang "We'll Bring the World His Truth"—truly a memorable experience! I felt gratitude that our four children had chosen to give missionary service and, interestingly, on four different continents—in Belgium, Korea, Washington, D.C., and Argentina.

One morning in 1999 as I was walking past the Provo Temple, I saw two young boys across the street in great distress. One was stuck halfway under the wrought iron fence of the temple grounds, and the other was desperately trying to pull his brother through the rest of the way. I could see they were on the edge of panic, so I ran across to help. After slightly calming the entrapped boy, we were able to back him out the way he came in. They were still somewhat upset, so I walked toward school with them to help them settle down. When I asked where they were from, they said, "We're from Africa, but we go to Pleasant View 9th ward!" I got their names and addresses and learned their father was studying at BYU Law School. When I asked if they knew the Primary songs, I got an enthusiastic yes in reply. I said, "Then let's sing 'We'll Bring the World His Truth.'" I couldn't help chuckling right out loud as Bokang and Mmusi Butandu skipped happily down Temple Hill singing at full volume, "We are as the army of Helaman, we have been taught in our youth . . ." It made my day!

Originally there were just three verses to this song, but at the request of the Primary General Board I added a fourth verse to complement the theme of a Primary sacrament meeting presentation. I have included that additional verse here.

We'll Bring the World His Truth
Words and music by Janice Kapp Perry

We have been born as Nephi of old
To goodly parents who love the Lord
We have been taught and we understand
That we must do as the Lord commands

Chorus
We are as the army of Helaman
We have been taught in our youth
And we will be the Lord's missionaries
To bring the world His truth

We have been saved for these latter days
To build the kingdom in righteous ways
We hear the words our prophet declares
"Let each who's worthy go forth and share"

Repeat Chorus

We know His plan and we will prepare
Increase our knowledge through study and prayer
Daily we'll learn until we are called
To take the gospel to all the world

Repeat Chorus

We are God's children, we have received
The blessings promised to Abraham's seed
We'll share the gospel, this is our quest
'Til every nation on earth is blessed

Repeat Chorus

❖   ❖   ❖

A Child's Prayer

A few of the songs I have written hold a particularly special place in my heart—"A Child's Prayer" is one of them. We are all human and occasionally wonder, in difficult times, if the Lord is really there to hear and answer our prayers. During one of my times of frustration over a seemingly unanswered prayer, I wrote a song called "Lord, Are You There?" I later decided to write a children's version, which I entitled "A Child's Prayer."

In my first version of the song the child asked "Heavenly Father, are you really there?" and the Lord answered, "Pray, I am here; speak, I am listening" in the counter melody. When the piece was chosen as one of the winners of the *Ensign* songwriting contest, I was taught by the Correlation Committee that only direct quotations from the Lord should be attributed to Him. They suggested having a parent or teacher sing the second melody with the words, "Pray, He is there; speak, He is listening." The suggestion was a good one, and it also meant the part could be sung by either a man or a woman.

I have received many touching letters through the years from people who have had sweet experiences with this song. One mother related that when her small child needed an MRI, they could not get him to lie still until she promised to entertain him with Primary songs. He said, "Okay, I'll go first," and then started singing "A Child's Prayer," which brought tears to the doctors' eyes. Another mother wrote that her son had broken off two back teeth and the dentist had tried for so long to get the roots out that the boy was completely unnerved.

The dentist felt he should send the boy home and try again later. The mother had a prayer with her son and then asked if he would let the dentist try once more while she sang "A Child's Prayer." The boy agreed, and the procedure was successfully completed. A woman from Phoenix said she had had her husband sing this piece for her in the final stages of her four childbirths! On the lighter side, a grandmother said that when her two-and-a-half-year-old granddaughter was asked to say the blessing on the food, she began "Heavenly Father, are you really there . . . "

I have heard this song performed in many settings, including funerals, and I recently sang it with my friends in the Tabernacle Choir at general conference. For that occasion, Brother Craig Jessop, associate director of the Choir, asked me to expand the song. Eight lines were added at the beginning to set the stage for the child's prayer, and a few lines were added to the ending.

I had a very personal experience with this song in July 1998. Just three days after my husband and I returned from the Tabernacle Choir's European tour, we were involved in a serious car accident in which the front of my throat was badly ruptured and was bleeding internally. At a time when I was finding it difficult to speak, swallow, and breathe, I was told by hospital personnel that I needed to lie flat and absolutely still for thirty minutes while a CAT-scan assessed the damage to my neck. I desperately searched for something to calm me emotionally. I closed my eyes and repeated these words over and over in my mind for the duration of the test: "Pray, He is there; speak, He is listening. You are His child, His love now surrounds you." Surgery and rest eventually healed my throat, but the words of the song calmed my spirit at a critical time.

A Child's Prayer

Words and music by Janice Kapp Perry

(First 8 lines added in 1998)

A. Adult

    Night time, quiet time
    Loved ones gather at day's end
    I hold them close, I help them know

That God will always be their friend
Then just before I say goodnight
My little one kneels by my chair
I close my eyes, I dim the lights
And listen to this simple prayer:

B. *Child*

Heavenly Father, are you really there?
And do you hear and answer every child's prayer?
Some say that heaven is far away
But I feel it close around me as I pray
Heavenly Father, I remember now
Something that Jesus told disciples long ago
"Suffer the children to come to me"
Father, in prayer I'm coming now to Thee

C. *Adult*

Pray, He is there
Speak, He is list'ning
You are His child
His love now surrounds you
He hears your prayer
He loves the children
Of such is the kingdom
The kingdom of heav'n

Sing Parts B and C Together

Sing Part D and E Together

D. *Child*

Heavenly Father, are you really there?
Please hear my prayer

E. *Adult*

He hears and answers
Every child's prayer

❖   ❖   ❖

His Image in Your Countenance

This piece came straight from the pressure cooker—no time to simmer slowly while the flavor developed! Ideally, I prefer having time to write, rewrite, and refine both lyrics and music, but in this case I had no such luxury.

I arrived in Greensboro, North Carolina, on a Saturday afternoon prior to my presenting a musical fireside in that stake on Sunday evening. I visited throughout the evening with my hostess, Judy Rawlinson, and just before I retired to my bedroom for the night she said, "Could you write a theme song for our Young Women's conference while you're here?"

"When is it?" I asked.

"Tuesday evening."

"But tomorrow is tightly scheduled, and I leave Monday morning—there is no time!"

"Well, just think about it," she insisted, and as she showed me to my room she said, "The theme is 'Inner Beauty/Outer Beauty.'"

Left alone in my room and weary from a day of travel, I pulled down the covers of the bed and gasped as I saw bright red-and-white striped sheets with these words inscribed on them in thick black permanent marker: "Janice Kapp Perry Slept Here!" I was so startled my first reaction was to quickly pull the covers back up to hide the words.

Then, kneeling by the bed covered by those sheets, I said a half-hearted prayer about the song and climbed into bed expecting to fall asleep immediately. Instead, the phrase "inner beauty/outer beauty" kept passing through my mind. I recalled having read the thought-provoking question in Alma 5:14 earlier in the day on the plane: "Have you received his image in your countenances?" I recognized the relationship of that question to the inner beauty/outer beauty theme and a light went on in my mind, causing me to sit up in bed, turn the lamp back on, and pick up pencil and paper to write the song that I knew was coming. Two hours later, at 2:00 a.m., I completed the words for the first verse and chorus of "His Image in Your Countenance." I switched off the light and fell asleep, leaving the ideas for verses 2 and 3 simmering in my subconscious. At 5:00 a.m. I awakened and stole out to the piano to write a simple accompaniment for the song.

Sunday was filled with church meetings, a family dinner, the evening fireside, and late-night visiting with Judy—no time to write more on the song.

Before catching the plane Monday morning, I left the piano accompaniment with Judy, which had verse 1 and the chorus penciled in. Between Greensboro and Chicago I wrote verse 2. Between Chicago and Salt Lake City I wrote verse 3. I called Judy from the Salt Lake City airport and read the two additional verses, which she then added to the music sheets I had left with her. A young woman from her ward learned the song that very day, and it was performed Tuesday at their Young Women conference!

The piece has been well-received through the years, proving, I guess, that there is more than one ideal way to write a song. Sometimes a short deadline and a little adrenaline, when enhanced by the Spirit, can produce a good result.

His Image in Your Countenance
Words and music by Janice Kapp Perry

With no apparent beauty that man should Him desire
He was the promised Savior to purify with fire
The world despised His plainness but those who followed Him
Found love and light and purity, a beauty from within

Chorus
Have you received His image in your countenance?
Does the light of Christ shine in your eyes?
Will He know you when He comes again
Because you will be like Him?
When He sees you will the Father know His child?

We seek for light and learning as followers of Christ
That all may see His goodness reflected in our lives
When we receive His fullness and lose desire for sin
We radiate His perfect love, a beauty from within

Repeat Chorus

The ways of man may tempt us and some will be deceived
Preferring worldly beauty, forgetting truth received
But whisp'rings of the Spirit remind us once again
That lasting beauty, pure and clear, must come from deep within

Repeat Chorus

By His everlasting image in your eyes?

In Quiet Grove

In 1985 our daughter, Lynne, was called to serve in the Washington D.C. Mission. She had planned on serving a mission for as long as I could remember and had not let anything distract her from that decision. When she asked me to write a song for her farewell, I spent considerable time thinking about what would be most appropriate for her.

Years earlier when she was a teenager I had stopped by her bedroom to say goodnight. She said, "Mom, everything hinges on Joseph Smith. If we believe he prayed in a grove of trees and that Heavenly Father and Jesus appeared to him, then everything else that followed has to be true. If not . . . "

I waited a moment for her to finish, but when she did not I asked, "And do you believe it happened?"

"I *know* it did, Mom. That's why I have to serve a full-time mission when I'm old enough."

I left her room that night having experienced one of the greatest joys parents can ever hope for—knowing that one of their children has been blessed with a burning testimony of the truthfulness of the gospel of Jesus Christ.

Now it was time for her to leave home and spend eighteen months sharing that testimony with all who would listen. I felt strongly that the most meaningful song for her farewell would say, "It was in quiet grove it all began, the gospel fullness was revealed to men. We share this message with all the world in love, because a boy inquired of God in quiet grove."

In Quiet Grove
Words and music by Janice Kapp Perry

It was in quiet grove it all began
When God and Jesus Christ appeared to man
Revealing precious truths so long withheld
It was a miracle that day
It was a time the world would not forget
That sacred day when earth and heaven met
When in response to Joseph's humble words
The gospel fullness was restored
And since that day . . .

Chorus
> Each worthy one is called to teach His word
> Until the time when ev'ry child of God upon the earth
> Has heard the gospel plan
> That was restored to man

I, too, have asked of God as Joseph did
That I might know the truth of all he said
In prayerful moments when my heart is full
He sends a witness to my soul
Lord, help me share these things that I believe
Lead me to humble hearts who will receive
Then let the Spirit through me testify
That some may find the narrow way
For I believe . . .

Repeat Chorus

It was in quiet grove it all began
The gospel fullness was restored to man
We share this message with all the world in love
Because a boy inquired of God in quiet grove

❖   ❖   ❖

More Than Friendship

In 1985 I combined business and pleasure on a trip to Delaware, Virginia, and North Carolina. The week was packed with heart-touching experiences that inspired the writing of this song.

My first responsibility was speaking at a stake Relief Society conference in Dover, Delaware. The sister who was in charge of music for the conference, Brenda Manning, was Delaware's Young Mother of the Year. The week before she had been in New York City competing for the national title when she and her husband Bill received the tragic news that their little daughter had drowned back home. I entered a very tender situation in that stake as friends and loved ones were grieving this great loss. After the conference the Mannings invited me out to their beautiful farm in Amish country, and I walked with them to the picturesque little pond where Julie had drowned. There they expressed their deep sorrow and also their strong testimonies of faith and trust in the Lord. In that moment of sharing, a deep bond of friendship was sealed between us.

My next stop was in Virginia, where I was to visit a myotherapy clinic in hopes of finding relief from a serious dysfunction that had developed with my left hand. Our daughter, Lynne, was serving in the Washington D.C. Mission, and with permission from her mission president I visited her for a few hours at her apartment in Burke, Virginia. Lynne had two companions at the time, and while they were running a few P-day errands, she and I took a walk through the sunny green woods behind her apartment. It was truly an idyllic hour as we walked and talked in that peaceful setting, sharing her mission experiences and my family news, and basking in the joy we felt at being together. After we fixed lunch we knelt together in her apartment, and she offered a sweet prayer of thanks and testimony that I will always remember. Then she and her companions took me to the medical facility where we said good-bye, trying valiantly to keep our pledge to part without sadness.

After a few days at the clinic I flew to Greensboro, North Carolina, where I renewed friendships and spoke at a stake fireside. While there I received a comforting priesthood blessing for my hand from stake president Joe Hamilton and stake patriarch Homer LeBaron. I felt wrapped in the love of those good southern Saints.

The next day, on the plane back to Utah, I considered how I might appropriately thank all those with whom I had shared such unique gospel experiences. A thank-you note didn't seem nearly enough so I wrote the words to the song "More Than Friendship" on the plane, finished the music at home, and sent copies back to Delaware, Virginia, and North Carolina. I was sure our deep feelings of friendship had been compounded by our shared love for our Savior Jesus Christ.

This song is a very personal expression, and I gathered my courage to sing it—the first time I had done so on any of our first forty albums.

More Than Friendship
Words and music by Janice Kapp Perry

I seem to feel more than friendship
When I am by your side
Why do I feel so deeply
From touch of hand and loving eyes?

The things we feel together
Are only understood
By those who share a hope in Christ
Thoughts of eternal brotherhood

Because I know you love Him
Because I love Him too
It deepens and refines my love for you

The mem'ries of tender moments
We share in mortal years
Will only be more precious
When we progress to holier spheres

Together we will greet Him
That sacred day above
So eager for His fellowship
Already knowing how to love

Because I know you love Him
Because I love Him too
It deepens and refines my love for you

Through the Spirit
I hope you comprehend
It's more than friendship I feel for you
My friend(s)

❖   ❖   ❖

My Mother/My Daughter

I cowrote this song in 1984 with my cousin Joy Saunders
Lundberg. A stake in northeast Provo was preparing a music
festival and requested a song that could be performed by a large

mother-daughter chorus. I loved the assignment, as did Joy, and we felt that a counter melody format would be a natural choice for the two groups.

I was the "middle generation" at this point of my life, still drawing great strength from my mother, Ruth Kapp, and great satisfaction from watching my daughter, Lynne, mature into a beautiful and capable young woman. I could still remember well the tender feelings I had at leaving my own childhood home in Oregon for BYU, and I could also see that that time of separation was fast approaching for my own daughter. Joy was experiencing very similar things and I'm sure our personal feelings are evident all through this song.

Joy and I attended the festival and heard the piece performed for the first time by a wonderful chorus of two hundred young women and forty of their mothers—a very moving experience.

Lynne and I often sang this song at home, but after she received her call to serve in the Washington D.C. Mission, we found the words were a little too close to home and we put the song away in the piano bench until she returned.

"My Mother/My Daughter" was performed by a group of about three hundred mothers and daughters on a Church satellite broadcast from Temple Square in 1997.

My Mother/My Daughter

Words by Joy Saunders Lundberg and Janice Kapp Perry
Music by Janice Kapp Perry

Mother (1st part)
> Sometimes when I see you, my daughter, my own
> My heart fills with love seeing how you have grown
> Your hands, once so small, have remained clean and pure
> Your heart filled with love helps my own soul endure
> The prayers that you speak give me faith to go on
> And the smile in your eyes gives me hope for the dawn
> Then I wonder why, and give thanks that I
> Was chosen to be your mother

Daughter
> I've watched you, dear mother, each day of my life
> I've seen how you smile through the joy and the strife
> I've needed your love and have known you were there

I've seen how you help to bring answers to prayers
The world that surrounds me is blind and unsure
But with you as my mother I'm safe and secure
Then I wonder why, and give thanks that I
Was chosen to be your daughter

Mother (2d part)

The seasons come, the seasons go, and I see you grow
The light of truth is in your eyes, I saw it long ago
I weep at your sorrows, smile when life is fair
I speak your name in each tender prayer
I know the time will quickly come when I must let you go
But seeds of truth within your heart were planted long ago
So reach for your dreams, for every good thing
Depending on my love, my dear daughter

Mother (2d part) and Daughter Together

Depend upon my love, my dear daughter/mother

❖ ❖ ❖

(Jesus Was) No Ordinary Man

In 1983 my cousin Joy Saunders Lundberg and I wrote and published a sacred cantata entitled *The Savior of the World*—a forty-minute presentation on the life and mission of our Savior, Jesus Christ. Our research for this work, and every scriptural reference used in the narration and music, were from the New Testament. Thus, we decided to submit the cantata to a large distributor of Christian music in the Midwest, hoping that people of all faiths might enjoy performing it.

The publisher, noting our Provo, Utah, address, returned our manuscript along with a terse letter which stated, "We do not consider Mormons to be Christians. We consider them a cult, and if we were to publish music written by Mormons, it would greatly damage our reputation!"

We were shocked. We had not known until then that many in the Christian world held this view of Mormons. We did not make any further effort to convince him to distribute our music, but we did compose a lengthy letter explaining to him that we are indeed Christians—we are The Church of *Jesus Christ* of Latter-day Saints; we pray in His name; we try in every aspect of our lives to emulate Him; He is the cornerstone of our religion!

We did not receive a response to our letter, but his words stayed in my mind and heart for some time and created within me a strong desire to write something that would affirm my testimony of the divinity of Jesus Christ.

I read, studied, and prayed about this subject for a few days before writing the song "(Jesus Was) No Ordinary Man." I felt a profound gratitude for having been born to parents who believed in His divinity and helped me to gain my own testimony of Him.

Many learned people in Jesus' own day who heard His teachings and witnessed mighty miracles were still deceived in their hearts, even to the point of crucifying Him. It is difficult to understand why they did not "sense His divinity and know from whence He came." "No Ordinary Man" is my personal testimony that He who was crucified was Jesus Christ, the Son of God, and Savior of the world.

Interestingly, a large publisher of Christian music from New York later heard our cantata *The Savior of the World* performed by the Mormon Youth Symphony and Chorus in the Salt Lake Tabernacle and asked to be granted publication and distribution rights for the work. He said, "I have had enough experience with Mormons to know you are Christians, but still I would not be foolish enough to *advertise* that it was written by Mormons!" He has marketed the cantata to Christian choirs for many years now.

(Jesus Was) No Ordinary Man

Words and music by Janice Kapp Perry

Chorus
>Jesus was no ordinary man
>But there were some who did not understand
>They saw Him working miracles

But some were still deceived
Why did they not believe?

When with few loaves and fishes the multitudes were fed
When He showed them His power to heal and even raised the dead
When He walked upon the water and He calmed the raging sea
Why did they not believe?

Repeat Chorus

When His faith filled the fish nets, gave sight unto the blind;
When they saw at His bidding even water turned to wine;
When He offered all He had to them if they would but receive
Why did they not believe?

Jesus was no ordinary man
The pow'r to bless and heal was in His hands
They saw him cleanse the leper
They saw him heal the lame
They must have sensed divinity
And known from whence He came
But understanding not His cause
They crucified the Son of God
And even then they did not understand
That Jesus was no ordinary man

❖   ❖   ❖

Song of Testimony

In 1980 I cowrote with my cousin Joy Saunders Lundberg a full-length musical entitled *It's a Miracle*. It was written and produced to encourage full-time missionary service among Church members, and all proceeds, above our expenses, were donated to the Missionary Department of the Church. At first we performed only in the western states, but in 1984 as momentum grew we planned a two-month United States tour that would bring our final performance total to 239 shows.

Our cast and crew of thirty set out across the United States on a bus named Faith and a truck named Works, carrying boxes

of the Book of Mormon, which we hoped to leave with new
friends along the way. We often performed in large civic audi-
toriums, where we were required to employ the services of
union stagehands. These seasoned and hardened old theater vet-
erans watched the youth and children in our cast throughout
our performance and backstage. They were often heard to say,
"We don't know what it is about these kids—there's something
different about them. Their faces are beautiful, they're well-
behaved, they love the people they work with," etc. Such com-
ments usually provided one or another of the young people a
perfect opportunity to give away a Book of Mormon, and not
one of them was shy about it. These stagehands didn't understand what they were seeing, but we did—the image of Jesus
Christ in the countenances of those who love Him and strive to
keep His commandments.

After one such experience, I spent a day or two of long travel hours on the bus writing lyrics that might answer the stagehands' question. Then, with a small portable keyboard on my
lap, I composed the musical setting for "Song of Testimony."

Song of Testimony
Words and music by Janice Kapp Perry

If you see the light of heaven in my eyes
If you see a joy that riches cannot buy
There's a simple explanation
That I freely share with all men
For this is where the priceless treasure lies

Chorus
> I know God lives, I know He loves me
> I know He hears me and He answers when I pray
> I know His son is my Redeemer
> And that He died for me that I might live eternally one day
> I daily drink of living waters
> For He has promised those who drink shall thirst no more
> I daily feast upon His teachings
> In perfect faith I grow because I know His promises are sure

If my countenance beams love in rich supply
If you sense a quiet peace and wonder why

If with open heart you'll listen as the precious truth is given
To these eternal truths I'll testify

Repeat Chorus

I know God lives, I know He loves me
He is my guiding light, my strength through all my days
This is my song of faith, my song of testimony,
My song of praise

❖ ❖ ❖

The Test

For fifteen years (1964 to 1979) I typed in my home for students and professors at Indiana University, Utah State University, and Brigham Young University to supplement our income. In 1979 I naively recorded in my journal: "I can't seem to control the index finger on my left hand while typing. I need to take a day off next week and have my doctor take care of it."

Thus began two decades of frustration, medical opinions and treatments, surgery, and therapies aimed at restoring control of my left hand. My wrist pulled under, as did my fingers, except my thumb and pinky. It was impossible to type and frustrating to pursue my new interest in writing music. I prayed fervently, had priesthood blessings, cried often, bargained with the Lord, and visited forty different doctors over the next five years but found no diagnosis or cure. It seemed the problem just appeared from nowhere to test and try me, and I did not pass with flying colors those first few years.

At the end of the fifth year I went to a blind osteopath, Dr. Iliff Jeffrey, to try physical therapy on my arm and hand. As he worked on me twice a week, I often complained about my problem, and he listened patiently. Then one day, in a truly defining moment, I realized the irony of my complaining to a *blind* man. I felt humbled and ready to be taught for the first time. Dr. Jeffrey, sensing the change in me, began to teach me about accepting this handicap more gracefully.

He explained that such things make us more dependent on the Lord, more humble in our prayers, and more trusting in the Lord's timing. He reminded me that there is a healing time for all the hurts of this mortal life, whether it be in this life or the next. Finally, he promised me that if I would endure this test with a humble heart, there would come a time when I wouldn't trade having the use of my hand again for all the important lessons I had learned from being without it.

This good doctor helped me greatly in my quest to find peace in this matter, and I wanted to write a song to honor him for his attitude of faith. The first verse of "The Test" was written specifically for Dr. Jeffrey. Verse 2 is for all who pray fervently for blessings that don't seem to come in the time and the way we had hoped they would. Verse 3 was added when I saw my cousin Lee Saunders struggle to find joy in life after the death of his wife, Lois, in a tragic accident.

Twenty years have now passed, and I can finally say that adversity has been my friend, teaching me things I could have learned no other way.

The Test

Words and music by Janice Kapp Perry

Tell me, friend, why are you blind?
Why doesn't He who worked the miracles
Send light into your eyes?
Tell me, friend, if you understand
Why doesn't He with power to raise the dead
Just make you whole again?
It would be so easy for Him
I watch you and in sorrow question why
Then you, my friend, in perfect faith reply

Chorus
>   Didn't He say He sent us to be tested?
>   Didn't He say the way would not be sure?
>   But didn't He say we could live with Him
>   Forevermore, well and whole
>   If we but patiently endure?
>   After the trial we will be blessed
>   But this life is the test

Tell me, friend, I see your pain
Why, when you pray in faith for healing
Does the crippling thorn remain?
Help me see, if you understand
Why doesn't He who healed the lame man come
With healing in His hands?
It would be so easy for Him
I watch you and in sorrow question why
Then you, my friend, in perfect faith reply

Repeat Chorus

Tell me, love, why must you die?
Why must your loved ones stand with empty arms
And ask the question why?
Help me know, so I can go on
How, when your love and faith sustained me,
Can the precious gift be gone?
From the depths of sorrow I cry
Though pains of grief within my soul arise
The whisp'rings of the Spirit still my cries

Repeat Chorus

❖ ❖ ❖

As Sisters in Zion

During the time the Church Music Committee was soliciting and evaluating hymns for the new hymnbook, our family was completely involved in writing, producing, and touring the United States with our missionary musical *It's a Miracle*. Thus I did not write or submit any hymns for consideration. Toward the end of the selection process, however, I received a letter from Brother Michael F. Moody, chairman of the Church Music Division, kindly offering me an opportunity to provide a musical setting for the hymn "As Sisters in Zion."

The three-verse text for this hymn had been extracted from a ten-verse poem by pioneer poet Emily H. Woodmansee, which was published more than a century earlier in *The Woman's Exponent* newspaper under the title "Song of the Sisters of the Female Relief Society." I was impressed that her words from way back then were still appropriate for women in the Church today.

Since the publication of the hymnbook, I have enjoyed hearing this hymn sung with enthusiasm in scores of stakes throughout the Church. Doug and I frequently speak at stake Relief Society conferences throughout the United States, and it is especially fun for me to hear *him* singing "As *sisters* in Zion we'll all work together . . . " with such conviction!

While touring back East with the company of *It's a Miracle,* I received an urgent request from Brother Moody to write an SSA version of the hymn for a women's chorus to sing on the Women's Satellite Broadcast from Salt Lake City. Our touring bus was broken down, parked in a weedy vacant lot in Philadelphia for repairs. When it became apparent we would be stranded there for a few hours, I realized that was my only chance to complete the arrangement quickly. I cleared away some weeds, sat on the ground, leaned against a fire hydrant, put my little battery-operated keyboard on my lap, and tried to block out the ugly surroundings and write something worthy of the Women's Satellite Broadcast—truly an experience in being *in* the world but not *of* the world. I mailed the arrangement to Salt Lake City later that evening.

Only in 2000 did I learn details about the wonderful pioneer poet Emily H. Woodmansee, with whom I had cowritten "As Sisters in Zion." After two separate speeches I gave in California, descendants of Emily and her sister Julia provided me with a wealth of information about the sisters, often written in Emily's own words. I was thrilled to learn her story.

Emily was born in 1836, the youngest of eleven children born to Thomas and Elizabeth Slade Hill in southwest England. She wrote, "Even as a child I was much concerned about my eternal salvation. . . . Hungry and thirsty for truth, I searched the scriptures. . . . Truly I was waiting for something, I knew not what" (Augusta Joyce Crocheron, *Representative Women of Deseret* [Salt Lake City: J. C. Graham & Co., 1884], 82).

At the age of twelve Emily heard the testimony of her cousin who had heard a new religion preached that claimed "God had spoken from the heavens to a man named Joseph Smith" (Crocheron, *Representative Women*, 83). Emily attended the next meeting and experienced a miraculous conversion from which she never wavered throughout her life. Julia, three years older, also embraced the gospel.

Emily was baptized at sixteen years of age and given a blessing in which she was promised she would "write in prose and in verse and thereby comfort the hearts of thousands" (Crocheron, *Representative Women*, 85). She and Julia sailed for America in 1856, traveled by rail from New York to Iowa, and pulled a handcart in the James Willie Company, enduring great hardship before reaching the Salt Lake Valley.

Emily bore one child in a plural marriage in which her husband deserted her. She then married Joseph Woodmansee and bore four sons and four daughters, endured many hardships, and remained faithful to the Church to the end of her life. She was a prolific poetess, writing hymn texts that appear in previous hymnbooks of the Church. Her unfailing faith in God's goodness is reflected in all her writing.

I hope she was allowed to observe as seven thousand women participating in the 2000 BYU Women's Conference service project in Cougar Stadium sang together her now-famous hymn text "As Sisters in Zion"—a direct fulfillment of the blessing she received in 1852.

As Sisters in Zion
Words by Emily H. Woodmansee
Music by Janice Kapp Perry

As sisters in Zion we'll all work together
The blessings of God on our labors we'll seek
We'll build up his kingdom with earnest endeavor
We'll comfort the weary and strengthen the weak

The errand of angels is given to women
And this is a gift that, as sisters, we claim
To do whatsoever is gentle and human
To cheer and to bless in humanity's name

How vast is our purpose, how broad is our mission
If we but fulfill it in spirit and deed

Oh, naught but the Spirit's divinest tuition
Can give us the wisdom to truly succeed

❖   ❖   ❖

How Great Shall Be Your Joy

In 1985 I received a request to compose a piece for a missionary homecoming. Because it would be used in sacrament
meeting, I based the song on two of my favorite missionary scriptures: Doctrine and Covenants 18:15 ("And if it so be that you
should labor all your days . . . and bring, save it be one soul
unto me, how great shall be your joy with him in the kingdom
of my Father!") and John 10:27 ("My sheep hear my voice, and
I know them, and they follow me.") The bridge of the song also
refers to John 21:15-17, in which the Lord asks three times of
Peter, "Lovest thou me?" and then instructs him, "Feed my
sheep."

During the writing of this song I reflected on my first experience in sharing the gospel with a close friend, my high school
teacher, Mary Redfield. I loved sports, and she was a great
teacher and a great friend. One evening after school as I helped
her grade papers, I felt a burning desire to tell her about the
Church and bear my testimony. I knew she was active in the
Methodist church, but I felt our friendship was secure enough
that I could share my "pearl of great price." I felt pretty shaky
when I first brought up the subject and she could sense my emotion, so she put her work aside and listened. It was the first time
I had ever borne my testimony or talked about the Church with
a nonmember. Suddenly I was on fire inside with the desire to
have her understand. When I had finished she said quietly, "This
means a lot to you, doesn't it?" We talked more, and she agreed
to visit our ward the next Sunday.

It was a fast and testimony meeting the first time she came,
and she was amazed at all the baby noise and happy talking
among the adults before and after the meeting. Still, she felt
something good and visited several times through the next

weeks. Eventually she agreed to have my Uncle Clarence Saunders, a stake missionary, give her the formal missionary lessons. To my great joy, after completing the lessons, she was baptized a member of the Church. As I stood by the baptismal font that day, I experienced a depth of joy that I had never known before—not even on the ball field!

The words "how great shall be your joy" came to mind forcefully. And as I considered her humble, receptive spirit, I remembered these words from the scriptures: "My sheep hear my voice, and I know them, and they follow me."

How Great Shall Be Your Joy
Words adapted from scripture by Janice Kapp Perry
Music by Janice Kapp Perry

Part One

    And if it so be that ye should labor
    All your days
    And bring but one soul unto me
    How great shall be your joy with him
    In the kingdom of our Father
    How great shall be your joy

Part Two

    My sheep hear my voice
    My sheep hear my voice
    And I know them, and I know them
    And they follow, they follow me
    They follow, they follow me

Parts One and Two Together

After Jesus had risen, He came to the sea
Asking three times of Peter
"Lovest thou me?"
"Yea, Lord," he answered
"Thou knowest I love thee"
Then Jesus commanded him
"Feed my sheep." My sheep

Repeat Parts One and Two Together

How great shall be your joy

I Walk by Faith

In 1985 I received a request from the Church to write a song that would name the seven Young Women values. The seven values were listed, and I attempted that evening to organize them into a set of lyrics. Having no success, I called Sister Ardeth Kapp, Young Women General President, and asked if I could write more general lyrics that would broadly cover the values but not list them specifically. In her kind way she said, "No, we need them to be listed *in order* so the song can help the girls remember them. *We* thought it looked difficult too, but we'll be praying for you!" She then explained the significance of the values and the fasting, prayer, study, and thought that had gone into developing the program over many months.

With my newfound understanding of my important assignment, I retired to my bedroom on a Sunday afternoon and asked my family that I not be interrupted for a few hours. I prayed with all the sincerity of my heart for guidance from the Spirit. I asked forgiveness for my shortcomings and recommitted my heart and soul to the Lord's service. I asked specifically that any unworthiness in my life would not prevent the song from being written. And then I set a blank page in front of me, picked up a pencil, and tried in every way I knew how to listen to the Spirit's prompting.

That warm, exhilarating feeling that writers yearn for (but which I have felt to this depth only a few times in writing hundreds of songs) came over me powerfully. What had seemed awkward and difficult two days earlier now seemed logical and possible. The words, including the preamble, were organized in just a short time, and the music came simultaneously.

It is rarely appropriate to share personal experiences of the Spirit, but this one was so significant to me that I would feel ungrateful if I did not acknowledge it. I felt that any writer in the Church who had been given this assignment might have written the *same* song.

"I Walk by Faith" was sung by Young Women around the world at the Worldwide Balloon Rising celebration (my son Steve referred to them as Helium's Warriors), and it was my great honor to conduct the girls from our region on the green hill below the Provo Temple.

In our travels through the world, I often hear Young Women singing this song. I feel deeply grateful to have had a part in helping them internalize these important values, and I honor Sister Kapp for recognizing that music helps the message to penetrate the soul.

I Walk by Faith
Words and music by Janice Kapp Perry

I will prepare to make and keep sacred covenants
Seek promised blessings of the priesthood through obedience
Live my life to claim the blessing sweet of exaltation
My testimony growing each new day

Chorus

    I walk by Faith, a daughter of heavn'ly parents
    Divine am I in Nature by inheritance
    The spirit whispers of mission, my Individual Worth
    So I seek for precious Knowledge, for learning and for growth
    I understand the meaning of Accountability
    Every Choice for good or ill is my responsibility
    I want to build the kingdom, and Good Works is the key
    By doing what I know is right I show Integrity.

I walk by faith, a daughter of heavn'ly parents
Divine am I in nature by inheritance
And some day when God has proven me
I'll see Him face to face
But just for here and now I walk by faith

Yes, just for here and now I walk by faith

❖   ❖   ❖

My Friend, My Brother

In 1983 our son Steve and daughter, Lynne, traveled to China to perform with the BYU Young Ambassadors. A young Chinese tour guide was assigned to travel on the bus with the YAs as they performed in different cities. The guide, Ge-yao Liu, was particularly befriended by Young Ambassador Rob Neeley, and Rob answered Ge-yao's questions about the gospel and even discussed the possibility of Ge-yao's attending BYU someday.

A short time after the YAs returned to Utah, Rob Neeley was tragically killed by a lightning strike. His wonderful parents did several things to honor Rob's life, one of which was to take up his cause of bringing Ge-yao Liu to BYU. That was not an easy thing to do, but they were determined, and eventually he did come.

Our family had some contact with Ge-yao during that first year as he became a star on BYU's International Folk Dance team. In his second year we invited him to live in our home, which he did for several years while obtaining bachelor's and master's degrees from BYU.

Ge-yao was taught the gospel through the efforts and testimony of the Neeley family and others, and eventually he decided to be baptized into the Church. Steve and I wanted to write a song for Ge-yao's baptism that would honor the friendship that began between Ge-yao and Rob in China and led eventually to Ge-yao's baptism here in Utah.

Steve and I worked together on the words and created the song so quickly we can no longer remember who wrote what. I do remember, however, how utterly sweet the emotion was at Ge-yao's baptism as Steve sang and Lynne accompanied this tribute to an eternal friendship . . . to be continued.

My Friend, My Brother

Music by Janice Kapp Perry
Words by Steven Kapp Perry and Janice Kapp Perry

My friend, my brother, I hope somehow you know
That seeds of truth you planted
On that day so long ago
Are growing strong and true within me
Even though you are gone
The gift of love lingers on
At times, my brother, I still can hear you say
The gentle words that touched me
On that long-remembered day

I found with you a lasting friendship
Now I wish you could know
How much your love helped me grow

Chorus
>   You never really say good-bye
>   To someone you have loved
>   A part of him will stay with you
>   And still remind you of
>   The way he cared
>   The things he shared
>   And how your heart believed
>   Your gift, my friend, will never end
>   The love lives on in me

My friend, my brother, the light within your eyes
Invited me to listen
And begin to realize
I am a worthy child of God
Deserving of heaven's love
Such simple words said so much
And so, my brother, I think of you this day
And in my heart I promise
I will come to you someday
And in the sweet embrace of brotherhood
How great our joy will be
If we endure faithfully

Repeat Chorus

My friend, my brother
The love lives on in me

❖   ❖   ❖

The Light Within

When I began writing music, one of my first assignments was to write a theme song for my stake's Young Women conference. "The Light Within" is one of the first pieces I wrote for the Provo Utah North Stake Young Women. The tradition continued for about fifteen years, even after we had moved from the original stake. These assignments were among my favorites.

Being given a theme and a deadline helps me focus my writing. The theme "The Light Within" suggested many things, but I find there is great power in setting the scriptures to music, so I settled on Doctrine and Covenants 84:46 as my focus: "The Spirit giveth light to every man that cometh into the world." Though we are all given that spirit of light, there are days when we forget to rely on it. We wander on our own until circumstances humble us and we recognize our need for seeking guidance through the Spirit.

This song later became the title song of one of our most successful albums.

The Light Within
Words and music by Janice Kapp Perry

"The Spirit giveth light to every man
That cometh to the world"
The Spirit shineth bright in everyone
That trusteth in the Lord
Life could be so easy
Fear would fly away
If I but choose to follow
The light of Christ each day
But there are certain times when I feel inclined
To find my way alone
There are lonely days when it's hard to pray
And I wander on my own
Then something brings me to my knees
"Dear Father," I begin
And suddenly I feel the light within

"The Spirit giveth light to every man
That cometh to the world"
The Spirit shineth bright in everyone
That trusteth in the Lord
I have felt His Spirit touch me as I pray
And I have felt Him lead me
When I have lost my way
And I am very sure when my heart is pure

He's with me every hour
When His perfect love comes from up above
I am filled with heaven's power
Then suddenly within my mind
The veil is very thin
I'm happy when I feel the light within

Yes, God will light the way for me
If I invite Him in
His Spirit is the light I feel within
His Spirit is the light I feel within

❖　❖　❖

And Whoso Receiveth You

In 1986 it was time to write a farewell song for our fourth, and final, child to serve a mission. The four had been called to missions on four different continents: Steve to Antwerp, Belgium; Robert to Seoul, Korea; Lynne to Washington, D.C.; and now John to Rosario, Argentina. There is something unsettling about the last child leaving home, and I wanted to find a scripture for the song that would comfort both him and me. I found the answer in Doctrine and Covenants 84:88—"And whoso receiveth you, there I will be also. . . . I will be on your right hand and on your left, and my Spirit shall be in your hearts, and mine angels round about you, to bear you up."

The first section of the song speaks of John's willingness to set aside his other life plans and devote himself to full-time missionary service for two years. The second section reminds the missionary of the Lord's promise to be on his right hand and on his left hand and to send His angels to bear him up—a very comforting thought to the missionary and to the parents who are concerned about his safety and well-being.

At the end of John's mission, Doug and I, along with Steve and his wife, Johanne, went to Argentina to visit all the major cities in his mission, presenting firesides for the Saints. President Guillermo Pitarch and his three eldest daughters traveled

with us (his wife had just had a baby three weeks previously
and remained in the mission home). It was a memorable experience. Best of all, however, we were able to be present as John
performed the final baptism of his mission—the Spirit was powerful, just as the scripture in the song had promised.

And Whoso Receiveth You

Words and music by Janice Kapp Perry

First Part
> In faith I heed the call to serve
> To share in love Thy sacred word
> My first desire Lord will ever be
> To worship Thee and to serve Thee
> I give my life to Thee
> A debt of gratitude to pay
> And by the Spirit I will now be led
> For I believe the words Thou has said:

Second Part
> And whoso receiveth you
> There will I be also
> I will be on your right hand
> I will be on your left
> My Spirit will be in your heart
> Mine angels round about you
> To bear you up
> To bear you up

Both Parts Together

Together
> Taking no thought for the morrow
> And the things I shall teach
> For my Father who is in Heaven
> Knoweth my needs
> And in that very hour it shall be given me
> The words I shall speak

Repeat First and Second Parts Together

For whoso receiveth you
There will I be also

A Time to Share

President Ezra Taft Benson once said that it is possible for women in the Church to "do it all"—they just need to do it in sequence. In Ecclesiastes 3:1 the Lord states it another way: "To every thing there is a season, and a time to every purpose under the heaven." One very important season for members of the Church is a time to share the gospel as a missionary.

"A Time to Share" was written for the mission farewell of Sister Carolyn Abe of Greensboro, North Carolina. Carolyn was a college graduate who was qualified to begin a career, but since she was not married at the time of her graduation, she chose to use that season to share the gospel with others on a full-time mission.

Those who skip this important season often feel regret in later years. Some highly successful LDS athletes who elected not to interrupt their athletic career to serve a mission have later expressed regret that they let that opportunity pass them by. On the other hand, I have never heard a promising athlete who *did* serve at the appropriate age express any regret, even though his later success in sports may have been diminished.

There is a natural rhythm and flow to our lives from birth to death, and each season is important. A newborn baby who is deprived of hugs, tender touches, and cuddling in its first few weeks may suffer severe emotional consequences; children have an optimal period of time for learning motor and language skills; at the age of eight children know right and wrong and may be baptized, and so on. The age of nineteen (for men) and twenty-one (for women) is a time to share the gospel and solidify their testimonies for life.

A Time to Share
Words and music by Janice Kapp Perry

God, in His wisdom, assigned a time and season
To every worthy purpose under heaven
Those who believe Him do all things in their season
Then blessings from His hand are freely given

Chorus
This is my season to leave the world behind
This is my season for helping others find

        The straight and narrow way
        That leads to joy beyond compare
        A time to learn, a time to love, a time to share

    Now is my season, and faith in Thee my reason
    For leaving all I know and love behind me
    Lord, I am willing to share the love I'm feeling
    That those who seek with honest hearts may find Thee

    Repeat Chorus

    When I'm discouraged I'll pray for added courage
    That in my work for Thee I may be fearless
    Some who will listen will witness through baptism
    They recognize the truth and feel Thy Spirit

    Repeat Chorus

    Trusting His wisdom, I dedicate this season
    To Him whose Holy name I proudly bear
    I give my heart and soul
    And thank Him humbly for
    A time to learn, a time to love, a time to share

                        ❖   ❖   ❖

I Love the Book of Mormon

As a freshman in high school I went to my bedroom on a
Sunday afternoon to begin my first serious reading of the Book
of Mormon. Seminary was not instituted in Vale, Oregon, until
after my high school graduation, so my Book of Mormon
knowledge came from my parents, grandparents, and Church
leaders. Nevertheless, I was so certain the Book of Mormon
was true, I felt almost embarrassed to ask. Just as some people seem to come to earth with certain dispositions of per-
sonality and temperament, I felt I came with a sure knowledge
of the truthfulness of the Book of Mormon.

I opened the book to First Nephi and began reading: "I,
Nephi, having been born of goodly parents . . ." At that point
I stopped, touched by the remembrance of the goodness of

my own parents and the great blessing it was to be born of goodly parents who loved the Lord and taught me the gospel. I picked up paper and pencil and, in the enthusiasm of youth, wrote: "I know my parents love me, and I'm always going to obey them." This simple statement has guided my life ever after and attests to the power of the Book of Mormon even in its first sentence. Obeying my parents was not always easy through my high school years, but in keeping my promise I came to feel, as I'm sure Nephi did, that obeying righteous parents felt good!

Since my marriage in 1958, I have read the Book of Mormon "with real intent" many times, often reading through the night because the burning in my heart would not allow me to sleep. After many such experiences I can say only that I still know the Book of Mormon is true. I wrote this song in an effort to condense my testimony into a few lines that could be set to music.

I Love the Book of Mormon

Words and music by Janice Kapp Perry

I love the Book of Mormon
It is the word of God
Preserved by ancient prophets
Who trusted in the Lord
I love the Book of Mormon
It is my sacred guide
It tells of life eternal
It testifies of Christ

Moroni made a promise
To those who seek the truth
If we will read and ponder
And ask of God in faith
The Holy Ghost will witness
The Book of Mormon's true
It offers peace in this life
And joy eternal too

❖　❖　❖

I Pray in Faith

During the year before the Church published the *Children's Songbook*, those in charge of selecting the songs asked me to write one or two more songs with counter melodies. They mentioned that the children seemed to enjoy this technique in "Love Is Spoken Here," and it provided a natural way for them to learn to sing harmony. They specifically asked that I write one that would teach children the four steps of prayer.

The first melody talks about the importance of daily prayer. The counter melody enumerates the four steps: 1) addressing Heavenly Father, 2) thanking Him for blessings, 3) asking for the things we need, and 4) closing in the name of Jesus Christ.

I believe that these instructions, simply stated and set to music, can help even very young children learn the correct way to approach Heavenly Father in prayer.

I Pray in Faith
Words and music by Janice Kapp Perry

First Part
    I kneel to pray
    Every day
    I speak to Heav'nly Father
    He hears and answers me
    When I pray in faith

Second Part
    I begin by saying
    "Dear Heavenly Father"
    I thank Him for
    Blessings He sends
    Then humbly I ask Him
    For things that I need
    "In the name of Jesus Christ
    Amen"

Sing Both Parts Together

❖   ❖   ❖

Just One Little Light

I received a request from Sister Ardeth Kapp to write a song for an upcoming Young Women satellite broadcast. The subject was the importance of being a light to the world. I stopped in Salt Lake City on the way to visit my brother in Brigham City, and Sister Kapp and I discussed the assignment.

My mind started working on the song immediately. When I reached my brother's home, I excused myself and went to a bedroom to ponder the subject. I knew by now that assignments from the Church bring with them extra help from the Spirit, and I was excited to begin.

The idea came immediately to write about the power of just one young woman who is willing to be a light. In my enthusiasm, I called Sister Kapp and said, "I think I have an idea!" She said, "Before you tell me, let me share the idea that occurred to me after you left my office. I believe we should focus on the power of just one young woman who is willing to be a light. What do you think?"

I couldn't answer immediately because of the lump in my throat. When I finally could tell her our ideas were identical, she replied, "Isn't it nice to know we receive our inspiration from the same Source!"

The next week I was sitting out in our carport puzzling over words to complete the song. A neighbor, Brad Burton, walked across the street and asked, "What are you so engrossed in?" I explained that I was feeling the pressure of writing a song that was good enough for all the young women in the Church to hear and sing. Brad, who is a psychologist, answered, "Just make it good enough for the young women of our ward, and it will be good enough for every girl in the world." That timely bit of wisdom helped me greatly then and in all my writing since. I finished the song and thanked the Lord for sending help from one of His angels disguised as my neighbor.

I was seated on the sixth row of the Salt Lake Tabernacle when a chorus of more than three hundred young women introduced this song on the satellite broadcast.

Just One Little Light

Words and music by Janice Kapp Perry

Each daughter of God born to the earth
Has the light of Christ within
A spirit that whispers of things to come
That whispers of where we began
Each daughter of God, through faith in the Lord,
Must find and nurture the light
Then stand as a witness for Jesus Christ
A beacon burning bright

Chorus

    Just one little light in the darkness
    Shining through the night
    Can grow to a flame of glory
    Setting the world alight
    If that one little light
    Is the pure love of Christ
    Kindled by faith in His word
    The flame will shine with a pow'r divine
    For He is the Light of the World!

Each daughter of God, filled with the light,
Keeps the torch of truth alive
Though storms may arise and the winds may blow
The flame of the torch will not die
For this is the light, eternal and true,
That shines and cannot be dimmed
The light of the gospel of Jesus Christ
A priceless gift from Him

Repeat Chorus

I will stand for truth and righteousness
The flame of faith burning clear and bright
I will hold it high through eternity
That all, beholding my light, will see
I seek for the truth
I live for the promise
I follow in faith
My faith is in God!

❖   ❖   ❖

When You Know

I wrote "When You Know" to be sung at the mission farewell of two young men in different parts of the United States and in very different stages of testimony and commitment to serve. Both young men received their mission call at the age of nineteen, both accepted their call and entered the Missionary Training Center, but only one was spiritually prepared to continue.

The first young man was from North Carolina. Because he had planned and prepared for his mission spiritually and in other ways, he completed his MTC training and left for the mission field.

The second young man was from Utah, from a wonderful LDS family, but was not yet strong enough in his testimony and commitment to serve a mission. He left the MTC after a short time and returned to his parents' home. To his great credit, over the next few months he prepared himself to return to the MTC with a strong testimony and desire to serve. He now knew the gospel was true. He said that "when you know," you have the desire and strength to go and serve with all your heart. This piece was sung at his farewell, also.

Both young men served honorable missions.

When You Know
Words and music by Janice Kapp Perry

Father, I give my life to Thee
Just as long ago my Savior gave His life for me
Suff'ring patiently upon the cross at Calvary
That He might pay the price for sin for me
Father, I've prayed in quiet hours
Just to feel the peace that comes through Thy redeeming pow'r
I have felt a sweet assurance deep within me grow
And I am filled with love for now I know

Chorus
    And when you know
    The light of heaven fills your soul
    Shining bright and clean for all the world to see
    I will let my light so shine that others seeing me
    Will find the straight and narrow way that leads to Thee

Father, remember now, I pray
Those whose love and faith have kept me in the narrow way
Walk beside me as I live my life in harmony
To honor them and thus to honor Thee
Father, I now desire to be
Thy disciple through my life and for eternity
I have felt the Holy Spirit speaking to my soul
Now I will serve in might because I know

Repeat Chorus

Father, I give my life to Thee
Just as long ago my Savior gave His life for me
Take my willing heart and let Thy blessings freely flow
And I will serve, dear Lord, in love, for now I know

❖   ❖   ❖

Birthday, Birthday

I have heard that the traditional birthday song "Happy Birthday to You" brings in a huge royalty to the copyright holder each year—not bad for a song with only four lines, three of which are identical! On the other hand, most of the world will never hear this new birthday song. And best of all, you can sing it to *yourself* if the world forgets to remember your special day.

"Birthday, Birthday" was born while I was working with Roger and Melanie Hoffman, Marvin Payne, and my son Steve on a children's series called *Scripture Scouts,* in which three children and their talking dog are exploring the scriptures together in their treehouse. Maybe you have to hear Roger's bubbly arrangement to feel the magic, but the song has always made me feel good.

Birthday, Birthday
Words and music by Janice Kapp Perry

Birthday, birthday, coming-to-earth day
Pink and wrinkled and small

Birthday, birthday, it was the first day
I was anyone at all
It isn't a day I remember
But I know it was happy, for I've been told
How my mother smiled
And held me tight
And welcomed me into the world

Birthday, birthday, coming-to-earth day
Pink and wrinkled and small
Birthday, birthday, it was the first day
I was anyone at all
I could cry and wiggle and sleep and goo
And that's about all I could do
But it's fun to imagine
The day when I was brand-new

Birthday, birthday, coming-to-earth day
This is how life is begun
Happy birthday everyone

❖ ❖ ❖

The Word of Wisdom

This two-part children's song was written specifically for the *Children's Songbook,* at the request of those compiling it. Though it seems very simple in its final form, I researched the subject extensively before attempting to reduce it to the simplest terms for the children.

The words for the first melody simply state that the Lord revealed the Word of Wisdom to his prophet Joseph Smith and that blessings are promised to those who obey these principles. The words for the second melody are from the writings of Elder John A. Widtsoe, who stated that those who obey the Word of Wisdom will receive the blessings of a clean body, a clear mind, and a spirit in tune with the Lord. Hopefully, the musical setting will plant the words deep in the hearts of the children.

The Word of Wisdom
Words and music by Janice Kapp Perry

First Part
> The Lord has revealed
> The Word of Wisdom
> To Joseph Smith
> The Prophet
> If we obey
> And follow in faith
> Beautiful blessings
> Are promised

Second Part
> A clean body
> A clear mind
> A spirit in tune
> With the Lord
> These are promised
> To all who follow
> The word and will
> Of God

Sing Parts Together

❖   ❖   ❖

Do Not Run Faster

As a new ward Relief Society president in 1988, I attended a regional training meeting conducted by Sister Barbara W. Winder, General President of the Relief Society. For three hours we were masterfully instructed on how to improve our Relief Society service. Each hour I felt more overwhelmed at the thought of implementing so many new ideas. I felt great relief at the conclusion of the final session when Sister Winder put things in perspective by suggesting we choose just one or two of the suggestions to work on, and, above all, "do not run faster than you have strength."

Of all the things I learned at that conference I clung most to that comforting advice from the scriptures. I pondered it for several days, trying to identify why it meant so much to me, and then composed a song to help me, and perhaps others, remember the principle. We later recorded the song on an album, and it came back to haunt me on a particularly busy day.

I had spent three hours on a Tuesday morning overseeing Homemaking meeting in our ward. I knew my mother was ill and felt that I *should* be with her; my little granddaughter Sarah had burned her hands and I *wanted* to go see her; my nephew Kyle had arrived from Alaska, and I had promised to help him complete his missionary shopping that afternoon before entering the MTC the next day; and I was hosting an open house for him that evening at our home for all the Utah relatives. I was going in so many directions I wasn't really doing justice to anything!

An hour before the open house, I realized I had forgotten something important that I needed for the refreshments, so I hopped into the car, switched on the radio (which was set on the LDS music station), and heard my song. As the singer reminded me, "Do not run faster than you have strength," I said (to the voice on the radio) in a very firm voice, "That's easy for *you* to say!"

Months later when I was talking to my doctor about feeling tired and run down, he said, "I often give my patients who are in your situation a copy of your song 'Do Not Run Faster'— maybe you should give it a listen!"

It is so important to concern ourselves with only the few things that really matter, do them the best we can, and have a measure of peace in our lives. Now, if only I can remember that next week . . .

Do Not Run Faster

Words and music by Janice Kapp Perry

I thought that I could do it all
Complete each task, accept each call
I never felt my work was done
Until I had pleased everyone
I told myself I must be strong
Be there for all to lean upon
But in the end I came to see

That's more than God requires of me
He has said:

Chorus

> Do not run faster than you have strength
> If you grow weary, what have you gained?
> You will have wisdom and strength enough
> If first you remember to fill your own cup

I thought of all I could become
Compared myself to everyone
I never stopped to keep the score
But always felt I should do more
I somehow thought I must become
Everything to everyone
But in the end I came to see,
That's more than God requires of me
He tells me:

Repeat Chorus

Comforting words of the Master
Do not run faster than you have strength

❖   ❖   ❖

First Christmas in Love

When your son is twenty-eight and in love at last, I believe
it calls for a song! Steve had met Johanne Fréchette years earlier when he had just returned from his mission and she was
enrolling for her freshman year at BYU. Both were members of
the BYU Young Ambassadors performing group, and as Steve
gave the opening prayer at the group's first meeting, Johanne,
who was a convert and had been told to keep her eye out for
returned missionaries, thought, "Wow, what if I married *him*?"

Because they were in different Young Ambassadors groups,
they worked together only occasionally and toured separately
to more than thirty countries over several years. During those
years Steve frequently expressed (to us) admiration for her talents and performing ability, but they only occasionally dated.

Johanne, on the other hand, had expressed to Doug and me that her feelings for Steve were more than just friendship and we thought her more than patient in waiting for him to respond with a commitment. Finally, after what we call "a whirlwind seven-year courtship," during which Steve finally came perilously close to losing her to a more ardent suitor, they became engaged and soon were married.

We loved to see the new spark in Steve's eyes and, especially at the time of his first Christmas in love, I couldn't resist trying to capture his happy mood musically. He and Johanne recorded this song on our family Christmas album.

First Christmas in Love
Words and music by Janice Kapp Perry

Are the lights a little brighter this year?
Is the snow a little whiter this year?
Is the glow from the fireplace as soft as it seems?
It wraps me with happiness, fills me with dreams

Is my step a little quicker this year?
Is my heart a little bigger this year?
Maybe nothing has changed, but it seems so because
It's my first Christmas in love

There is magic in the music this year
There is joy in every carol I hear
All the sweet Christmas feelings, the sights and the sounds
Are somehow more wonderful this time around

Is my smile a little brighter this year?
Is the world a little righter this year?
Maybe nothing has changed, but it seems so because
It's my first Christmas in love

All the wonders of Christmas have been there before
But this year it seems to mean so much more

It's our first Christmas in love
It's the best Christmas that ever was!
Through the years we'll remember this season because
It was our first Christmas in love

Spoken: Isn't that the mistletoe?

Jessica Noelle

Imagine our joy when we learned that our first grandchild was due on Christmas Day of 1987! Of course, babies rarely arrive on their due date, but just anticipating a baby in the Christmas season was exciting. We watched eagerly as the weeks and months passed, leading to this new season of our lives. We were more than ready to be grandparents and looked upon this event as the ultimate Christmas gift.

When Christmas Eve came with no signs of an imminent birth, and after the doctor said to the expectant mother, "We'll check you again in a week," we all settled in for the wait. But then the call came from our son Robb at seven o'clock Christmas morning: "Mom, we're at the hospital, and they're not sending us home!"

Instantly, this Christmas held an excitement unequalled by any Christmas past. Robb called with progress reports throughout the day, and we gamely tried to proceed with our usual Christmas morning routine. But we were so excited we could hardly open gifts in any sane fashion. Each phone call from the hospital sent the adrenaline pumping, and the final call at three o'clock in the afternoon announcing the arrival of Jessica Noelle Perry was a moment of intense happiness for us. (We knew they planned to name a daughter Jessica, but Noelle was added because of her timely Christmas arrival.)

We quickly drove across town to the hospital and raced to the nursery for our first view of Jessica. This new grandma could not hold back the tears as we first saw her through the nursery window, *au naturale,* kicking and crying and looking strangely familiar. I was truly in awe of the whole experience.

Our granddaughter's name—Jessica Noelle—was a song title if ever I had heard one! I began forming lyrics for a Christmas calypso by that title.

Jessica Noelle

Words and music by Janice Kapp Perry

One Christmas morning we still recall
Came to us the best gift of all
Our son called early that joyous morn
To say our first grandchild would be born

We opened presents from Santa Claus
Light with laughter and joy because
We were waiting so happily
Wondering who the baby would be
And she was . . .

Chorus

> Jessica Noelle!
> Christmas angel from heaven fell
> Jessica Noelle!
> A Christmas story we love to tell
> Light the Christmas tree, ring the bell
> Welcome little Jessie Noelle!

We traveled quickly that wint'ry day
To the place where the baby lay
We looked in wonder, we gazed in awe
At the little stranger we saw

They placed the baby within our arms
Tears were falling now, soft and warm
No one can measure, no words can tell
Of the perfect love that we felt
As we held . . .

Repeat Chorus

Our Christmas angel was born to earth
The day we celebrate Jesus' birth
And through the years we will all recall
The most merry Christmas of all
With little . . .

Repeat Chorus

❖   ❖   ❖

A Child Again

I have met many people throughout my life who lead very lonely lives—some who have been ostracized by their peers, some who never marry, some who have lost their spouses through death or divorce, and so on. I have heard some of these friends say that there is a place in their minds to which they occasionally retreat for comfort—perhaps an earlier time in their lives when they felt love, security, and peace.

I am most grateful for the shared insights of a single friend who, though she lives a busy, productive life, occasionally has a strong sense of something important missing in her life. She finds comfort recalling childhood days when there were loving arms around her, saying "everything's all right." Ultimately, she finds solace through praying to a loving Father, who will always be her refuge and her friend.

A Child Again
Words and music by Janice Kapp Perry

To the world it may seem my life has everything
But at times there's something missing that I never can explain
I often look behind me, but I always look in vain
No footsteps there, no one to call my name,
And I close my eyes against the lonely pain

Chorus
> And I'm a child again
> Loving arms around me, saying everything's all right
> Just a child again
> Crying out for someone to protect me in the night
> I hide from all the grown-up pain
> Pretending life's a childhood game
> I reach for someone's hand as I did then
> And I'm a child again

There are days when it seems my life is just a dream
And I'm looking through a window that's misty from the rain
I listen in the distance for a sweet, familiar strain
No sound is heard, no comforting refrain,
And I close my eyes against the lonely pain

Repeat Chorus

But no one's there to hear my call, I'm really not a child at all
The dream is gone and now I must go on
So I pray for help from Father, and as I say "Amen"
I know He'll be my refuge and my friend
And upon His love I can depend

> And I'm His child again
> Loving arms around me, saying everything's all right
> I'm His child again
> Knowing there is someone to protect me in the night
> And He will always be my friend
> With Him I never need pretend
> He knows my heart and I am safe with Him
> And I'm a child again
> His child again

❖   ❖   ❖

An Early Good-bye

A funeral service for a person who has lived a long and productive life is often a solemn but joyful celebration of the goodness and completeness of his or her life. With the untimely passing of a younger person, however, the pain of unanswered questions, unfulfilled dreams and empty arms can be devastating. Loved ones, through faith, usually recover, because they *must,* but first they must deal with the pain of an early good-bye.

My first personal experience with the death of a young person was very traumatic. It happened when I was about twelve years old and visiting my friend Delma Grigg for the day. Her father, Nephi Grigg, was bishop of our ward in Vale, Oregon.

A couple who lived on a farm near ours, the Gardners, suddenly burst through the door of the Grigg home, crying "Bishop! Bishop! Our son Harvey [age eleven] has been killed!" Delma and I were frozen in fear in a corner of that room as the parents moaned and cried out in a terrible kind of grief that I had never seen or even contemplated before. Later, of course, comfort came. But seeing grief so fresh and overwhelming is something I have never forgotten.

More than forty years later that experience came back to me forcefully when my cousin David Ross called to tell me that the two teenaged sons of his good friends Clayton and Nita Kearl had been killed in a terrible car accident. I was heartbroken for them. I could not even imagine the depth of their grief. The next day David called to say the Kearls had requested that I sing "The Test" at their sons' funeral. I knew it would be a well-attended service with a General Authority present, and I didn't feel I could do it because of my emotions and my untrained voice. But a request to sing at a funeral is one you do not turn down, so I gathered my courage, asked my daughter, Lynne, to sing with me, and we did our best. The service was beautiful and comforting, and I marvelled at the Kearls' composure and strength. Still, I knew there would be days and years or even a lifetime ahead of mourning their loss.

At home a few days later I tried to imagine their tender feelings as I wrote a song for them, trying to describe the pain of an early good-bye.

An Early Good-bye
Words and music by Janice Kapp Perry

There is pain in an early good-bye
There are so many dreams you must set aside
So many mem'ries to cause you pain
So many plans to change
There is pain in an early good-bye
There are so many times when you question why
So many feelings you must deny, so many tears to cry
There are so many things that I wanted to say
So many reasons I hoped you could stay
I loved you completely, I have no regrets
But I just wasn't ready yet

So I'll cry a little bit, and I'll die a little bit
And I'll try with all my heart to make some sense of it
And there's only one Power to lean upon
There's only one reason that I can go on

I believe in the wisdom of God
He ruleth the seasons, he fails us not
This kind of sorrow He too has known
I do not walk alone
There is nothing and no one to blame
And there's no use in thinking what might have been
I would have kept you through life's short span
But God had a different plan
So I'll pray for the day when the sorrow will cease
Pray for the day when I'll know perfect peace
I'll find the courage to make it somehow
But I'm feeling so lonely now

So I'll cry a little bit, then I'll try a little bit
And I'll trust in God above to make some sense of it
Then my eye will be single to one bright star
To live my life worthy to be where you are

But today it's not easy, today I may cry
So if you see a tear in my eye
It's the pain of an early good-bye

❖   ❖   ❖

Be Still, and Know That I Am God

"Be still, and know that I am God," a simple but powerful passage from Doctrine and Covenants 101:16, can bring comfort in every kind of trial as we realize that one far wiser and stronger than we are is watching over the circumstances of our lives.

Our serious trials usually bring us to our knees imploring the Lord for understanding that can help us cope and find peace once more. Verse 1 describes that struggle in which we eventually hear (or feel) the faintest whisper, "Be still. . . . " Verse 2 describes the comforting feeling that our prayer is heard and that the Lord is aware of our distress. In verse 3 we arise from our knees with the assurance that He who has borne *all* sorrows understands our pain and will bless us in His own time and in His own way.

After writing the song in a time of personal turmoil, I bought a little card that had these comforting scriptural words imprinted on it and laminated it. Through the past decade I have pulled that little card out of my purse on many occasions and received instant comfort, just from having these words pass through my mind: "Be still, and know that I am God." I feel an instant laying of my burden at His feet.

Be Still, and Know That I Am God
Words and music by Janice Kapp Perry

In times of deepest trial
I plead to find relief
On bended knee I seek Thee
And pray I may find peace
And in that darkest hour
Comes the solace I have sought
I hear the faintest whisper
"Be still, and know that I am God"

I raise my eyes to heaven
I feel Thy presence near
And know that One who loves me
Has heard my searching prayer
Then gently Thou reminds me
Life's battles must be fought
I hear Thee now more clearly
"Be still, and know that I am God"

I rise with sweet assurance
My pain to Thee is known
Thou knowest of my suff'ring
I do not walk alone
Thy perfect love has healed me
Because I have been taught
By One who bore all sorrows
"Be still, and know that I am God"

❖　❖　❖

I Will Always Obey

I grew up with a natural disposition to obey my parents, which greatly blessed me throughout my life. I was safe in obeying them because they were loving followers of Christ who did their best to keep His commandments and asked only that I do likewise. My inclinations were in harmony with theirs, and our relationship was peaceful.

Conversely, I noticed that some of my friends who were also children of righteous parents suffered unhappy consequences from going against parental counsel. I wanted to write a song to express my deep feelings on this subject. I chose as examples of obedience our Savior Jesus Christ, the Prophet Joseph Smith, and the Book of Mormon prophet Nephi. All three obeyed the will of God and brought about magnificent blessings for all mankind.

While speaking in a stake in Idaho I mentioned I was writing a song on the importance of obedience. A woman in the congregation spoke to me afterward with a passion born of the parental abuse she had suffered as a child. She thought it extremely important not to advocate blind obedience, because some parents make unrighteous requests of their children. This idea was foreign to my own experience, but I had read and heard enough to know her advice should be given consideration. Thus I added the final lines to the song to clarify what kind of counsel children should obey. The song was published in the *Friend* in 1997.

I Will Always Obey
Words and music by Janice Kapp Perry

Jesus obeyed His Father
Kept His commandments perfectly
Even when He had to suffer and die
He did not murmur or question why
He knew the plan and He followed in faith
Jesus always obeyed

Joseph obeyed the Father
Followed directions faithfully

Seeing a vision he could not deny
He did not murmur or question why
He only listened and followed in faith
Joseph always obeyed

Nephi obeyed his father
Followed instructions carefully
Always so ready and willing to try
He did not murmur or question why
He only listened and followed in faith
Nephi always obeyed

When Heavenly Father speaks to me
Through parents or prophets or in quiet ways
I want to listen and follow in faith
I will always obey

❖   ❖   ❖

I Will Come unto Christ

The text for "I Will Come unto Christ" was written by Rodney Turner, my former bishop, a retired BYU religion professor, and poet supreme. It was the first of many collaborations
between us on songs, hymns, and a sacred cantata.

In 1989, members of our Provo ward planned a trip to Israel
under the auspices of BYU Travel Study, which was headed by
ward member George Talbot. Rodney Turner was to be our tour
guide, instructing us at important sites each day. Just before our
departure he brought me the text "I Will Come unto Christ," and
I was moved to tears by its beauty. I knew I must give it a hymn
setting before the trip.

Our tour was glorious. Our spiritual feelings increased with
every beautiful on-site lecture and culminated in an unforgettably sweet experience at the Garden Tomb. One real highlight
occurred on a warm, sunny afternoon on the Mount of Beatitudes overlooking the Sea of Galilee. In that idyllic setting we
heard Rodney Turner's tender story of the Beatitudes, and then
I handed out copies of the new hymn to tour members. I played

a cassette accompaniment to teach them the music, and we all sang the hymn together. The perfect setting and the beauty of the hymn created a memory to last for a lifetime.

After the trip, I entered the hymn in the *Ensign* hymn-writing contest. As a winner it was performed by a choir in the Assembly Hall on Temple Square the following year. I have never heard a hymn text before or since that moves me as this one does.

I Will Come unto Christ

Words by Rodney Turner
Music by Janice Kapp Perry

I will come unto Christ, who calls to me
As others were called by that ancient sea
Whose shores He walked in Galilee
When once He taught the blind to see
The ones who were blind like me

I will look unto Christ—let come what may—
In all that I do and in all I say
For He's the Potter, I, the clay
And I will serve Him day by day
And walk in the narrow way

I will sing the dear Lord's redeeming song
Of infinite love for the human throng
Of blood and tears shed for each wrong
Of hope made bright for all who long
To sing His redeeming song

I will honor the Father's Holy One
Redeemer of stars and of moon and sun—
Of kingdoms, glories He has won
For great and small when judgment's done—
All praise the Beloved Son

❖ ❖ ❖

Jesus, Listening, Can Hear

Years ago, I received a letter from Karen Smithson in Oregon telling me about her sister, Joyce Erickson, the mother of six children, three of whom were profoundly handicapped. Her letter was full of admiration and love for her sister, Joyce, and the way she devoted her life to the care of these children, who required so much extra time, energy, and love. She asked if I would consider writing a song to honor her sister.

Shortly after I received that letter, an article in the *Ensign* magazine caught my attention. Entitled "Jesus, Listening, Can Hear," the article was written by Jean Ernstrom, the teacher of a handicapped child named Heather. The story she related touched me deeply. Heather, who was unable to speak, had somehow communicated to her Primary teacher that she had a favorite song. After searching through the Primary book and other music, they finally discovered her favorite song was from the hymnbook: "There Is Sunshine In My Soul Today." And her favorite phrase within that hymn was "Jesus, listening, can hear the songs I cannot sing." What profound meaning that phrase would have for someone who could not communicate thoughts through speech or singing. I could not get the story out of my mind, and I determined to write a song for Heather and others who might feel as she did.

Shortly after the appearance of the *Ensign* article and while I was writing the song, I received another letter from Karen Smithson bringing the *Ensign* article to my attention and telling me that the little girl, Heather, who was mentioned in the article was one of her sister's three handicapped children.

As I wrote the song, I tried to put myself in the place of Heather or any other person unable to communicate testimony or gospel feelings. It must be extremely frustrating to have those beautiful spiritual feelings but have no way to express them. And yet, how comforting it must be to know that the Lord knows the thoughts of our heart and that silent testimonies can be borne and heard by the Lord—"Jesus, listening, can hear the songs I cannot sing."

When the song was completed, I sent a copy to the Ericksons for Heather and their other children. Sister Erickson called to invite me to attend a sacrament meeting on testimony bearing, in which Heather would be on the stand while her Primary teacher sang the new song in her behalf. I was eagerly looking forward to that day, but not long afterward a phone call from Sister Erickson gave me the news that Heather had passed away unexpectedly. Now the song would be sung by her teacher at her funeral service.

It was a sobering morning, listening to that touching, faith-filled funeral service for a courageous little girl. I felt so grateful that I had responded to the Spirit's prompting to write that song for Heather, which was now lovingly performed by her teacher as Heather's final earthly testimony.

Jesus, Listening, Can Hear
Words and music by Janice Kapp Perry

God did not give me voice to speak
And yet my faith is quite complete.
When I pray I have no fear,
For in my mind the words are clear.
And Jesus, listening, can hear.

He did not give me voice to sing,
But in my heart sweet music rings.
Melodies that no one hears,
Rise from my soul to heav'nly spheres,
And Jesus, listening, can hear.

I cannot speak to testify,
But faith shines brightly in my eyes.
In my heart it's very clear
The testimony I would bear,
And Jesus, listening, can hear.

When I need to feel Him near,
I think His name through silent tears,
And Jesus, listening, can hear.

❖ ❖ ❖

Just When I Need You

Most everyone in times of serious crisis finds it natural to cry out to the Lord in heartfelt prayer. When it seems there is truly nowhere else to turn, it is our instinct to seek a God we may have neglected or even forgotten during more peaceful and prosperous times.

This song was written more about the in-between times when we are striving to do what is right but make mistakes that discourage or depress us and even make us feel unworthy to approach our Father in Heaven in prayer. The thought that we are unworthy to pray does not come from God, for He would have us "come unto him" in every circumstance of our lives. In fact, the times when we are down on ourselves are precisely when we need most to seek the Lord's forgiveness and help. "Just When I Need You" was written while I was serving as ward Relief Society president and saw so many sisters struggling with feelings of discouragement and low self-esteem.

I have heard only one live performance of this song, but the circumstances made it very memorable. Through our foster son Mark Miner we were invited to provide a few musical programs at the Draper and Gunnison, Utah, prisons. After one such program we were informed that the inmates had a surprise for us. We were invited to sit on the front row of the congregation while a choir of about twenty men sang for us. They had a very capable pianist who, we were told, had made a choral arrangement of one of my songs. I was quite curious to see what they had chosen.

I felt many unexpected emotions during the next few minutes as they sang these words:

There are times when I'm almost overcome
By the thoughtless words I've spoken
And the foolish things I've done
And I want to say I'm sorry, and I even want to pray
But pride and shame get in my way

By the time they sang the words of the chorus—"Lord, just when I need you the most, I find it the hardest to let you know"—there were tears in the eyes of some of the singers and a real feeling of empathy in my heart for all their struggles and trials, which are not that different from our own. I never hear that song without remembering how meaningful the words were in that unusual setting.

Just When I Need You
Words and music by Janice Kapp Perry

There are times when I'm almost overcome
By the thoughtless words I've spoken
And the foolish things I've done
And I want to say I'm sorry, and I'd even like to pray
But pride or shame get in my way.

Chorus

    Lord, just when I need you the most
    I find it the hardest to let you know
    Just when I'm aching inside to be heard
    I can't seem to speak the words
    It seems when I'm down on myself
    I find it the hardest to ask for help
    Weak and unworthy I try to look up
    But cannot find strength enough

There are times when I seem to lose my way
And I'm burdened with the sadness
And the sorrow of the day
So I search beyond the shadows for a little ray of light
To lead me safely through the night

Repeat Chorus

Just when I'm feeling the pain
Give me the courage to call your name
I'll be down on my knees
Saying, "Help me, Lord, please
Help me to know you are close
Just when I need you the most."

❖ ❖ ❖

Lord, I Worship Thee

For about a decade I have written a song at Christmastime to send to friends as a Christmas card. I was pondering what to write in 1989 but never found time to do it. I suddenly realized that Christmas was almost here and I had been so caught up in all the shallower aspects of Christmas—gift buying, tree decorating, baking, cleaning, and so forth—that I had not reflected on the true spirit of Christmas so I could write a meaningful song.

One morning I felt so completely stressed out that I said to myself, "That's it! I'm going to get away from this routine and spend some time alone." I left a note for my husband saying I'd be back in the evening and headed for our cabin in Hobble Creek Canyon.

It is totally quiet and peaceful there, and while the cabin was warming I bundled up and took a much-needed nap. Then I read the Christmas story from the book of Luke and pondered it. I thought about the sweet parts of Christmas that I truly did enjoy—the lights, the bustle, the music, the family get-togethers—but I longed sincerely to feel the deeper meaning of the season. I prayed to feel my Savior's love and to find words to express my love for Him. I suddenly felt the peace I had been seeking, and I took pen and paper and wrote from my heart, "Lord, I Worship Thee."

Lord, I Worship Thee
Words and music by Janice Kapp Perry

I love to see the friendly sights of Christmas
The shoppers and the presents by the tree
But every year I like to pause
Far from toys and Santa Claus
To ponder what His coming means to me
To speak these gentle words on bended knee
"Lord, I worship thee"

I love to hear the happy sounds of Christmas
The music of the season touches me
But I must find a quiet place
Far from noise and hurried pace

To offer praise to heaven privately
To sing my song where only He can see
"Lord, I worship thee"

I love the way the world feels at Christmas
The happy crowds are beautiful to see
But also I need time to dream
Far from worldly Christmas scenes
To close my eyes and feel Him near to me
To cov'nant once again so willingly
"Lord, I worship thee"

❖　❖　❖

My Heart Sang a Lullaby

As struggling graduate students at Indiana University in 1968, my husband, Doug, and I were looking forward to a rather bleak prospect of Christmas gift-giving. We were, however, feeling excitement at the expected arrival of our fifth child in February.

Two weeks before Christmas a blood test revealed that our baby was in serious trauma from the effects of the Rh-factor, and probably would not survive long without our trying drastic measures. Doctors performed an intrauterine transfusion—a procedure in which whole blood plasma was injected through my abdomen into the baby's abdomen in hopes of sustaining the baby's life for a few more weeks.

The procedure seemed to be successful, but the next morning labor started prematurely, and a three-and-one-half-pound baby boy was born to us at eight o'clock that evening. We were comforted to hear his cries as he was born, but he was extremely ill, and doctors took him from us quickly to perform blood exchanges and other life-saving measures.

When everything possible had been done for him medically, Doug placed his hands on the baby's head in the tiny incubator and gave him a father's blessing and the name of Richard Scott Perry. Then we watched and prayed through the night.

At five o'clock the next morning, Richard died. Doug wrapped him in a tiny white blanket and brought him to my hospital room where we held him and prayed for comfort—a moment engraved in both our memories, a time when the words "born under the covenant" came to have new meaning.

Later, at home, Doug gathered our four children together for a special home evening to tell the story of a baby who needed to live on earth only briefly but who would always be a very real part of our eternal family.

Almost twenty years later, when it had become natural for me to express important life events musically, I relived the details of this poignant experience in writing this song. Tears flowed freely during the week I was writing the song, in what felt like a delayed grieving. Perhaps at the time of Richie's death I had been too busy comforting and reassuring our children to allow myself to grieve honestly. At any rate, writing and singing the song was very therapeutic, even all those years later.

There seemed to be a reverent hush in the recording studio as our daughter, Lynne, only one month away from the birth of her own child, relived this memory for us in singing "My Heart Sang a Lullaby."

My Heart Sang a Lullaby
Words and music by Janice Kapp Perry

Richie was born on a day in December
I know it was Sunday, some things you remember
Richie's first cries were like music to me
But no one could promise how long he would stay
And the night seemed so long
As we watched him and prayed

Chorus
    And my heart sang a lullaby to celebrate birth
    As he crossed the veil between heaven and earth
    My heart sang a lullaby for this tiny one
    A song of forever, of things yet to come
    Just a lullaby to carry him home

Richie was gone by the light of the morning
Before his first sunrise, before the day's dawning

So still in our arms, it was our turn to cry
A memorized moment as we said good-bye
And he looked like an angel
In his blanket of white

Repeat Chorus

Richie, my son, only here for a moment
He came, and he went, and the world didn't notice
But nothing's the same, especially for me
Eternity's promise is clearer to see
He has just gone ahead
To where I'll someday be

Repeat Chorus

Yes, a lullaby to carry him home

❖ ❖ ❖

On Earth As It Is in Heaven

When I hear the Lord's prayer spoken or sung I am especially touched by the phrase "on earth as it is in heaven." Everything I have been taught leads me to conclude that all the beauties and wonders that we enjoy here on earth will only be magnified in heaven. Brigham Young, for instance, said that when we hear the music of heaven, we will be overwhelmed.

Although it is impossible for us to see beyond the veil to these sublime beauties at present, certain earthly experiences are so overwhelming in their sweetness that I wonder if I am not receiving a brief glimpse of heaven. I feel it especially when witnessing the spectacular beauties of nature (such as those at the Washington, D.C. temple grounds), the soothing sounds of inspired music (singing "Come Thou Fount of Every Blessing" with the Tabernacle Choir), the whisperings of the Spirit (speaking peace in times of heartache), and the healing hand of a loved one when I am ill (priesthood blessings). "Many things that I hold dear, witness that God's love is here on earth as it is in heaven."

On Earth As It Is in Heaven

Words and music by Janice Kapp Perry

There is heaven all around us
If we have eyes to see
The miracles of nature
All witness quietly
That God created beauty here
To show us it could be
On earth as it is in heaven

There is heaven all around us
If we have ears to hear
The soothing sounds of music
Can quiet earthly fears
And bring a peaceful harmony
That often can be here
On earth as it is in heaven

There is heaven all around us
We find it on our knees
The whisp'rings of the Spirit
Are as a symphony
That plays within each yearning heart
Confirming peace can be
On earth as it is in heaven

There is heaven all around us
If we have heart to feel
The touch of one who loves us
Has pow'r to soothe and heal
For somehow in a caring friend
We see God's love revealed
On earth as it is in heaven

Many things that I hold dear
Witness that God's love is here
On earth as it is in heaven

❖   ❖   ❖

The Sun Comes Up inside of Me

In 1989 Joy Lundberg and I wrote and recorded an album of songs for youth entitled *Songs to Lean On*. We cowrote nine of the songs but needed one more to complete the album. I called Ardeth Kapp to ask what she considered the most important subject we could write about in that final song. Without a moment's hesitation she said, "I wish there could be a song that teaches youth the joy they can bring into their own lives by serving others." That was a subject I was very interested in, so with Joy's permission I wrote both words and music for this one.

I began by recalling countless times in my life when serving someone else had made *me* feel better and happier. In trying to put that feeling into words, I came up with the title phrase "The Sun Comes Up inside of Me."

When my mother died in 1991, I experienced that feeling at a time when I needed it badly. Mother had bone cancer and dealt with many challenges her final year. For a few weeks after her death I felt at peace, knowing she had been relieved of her infirmities, but then I began to grieve more, cry more often, and feel depressed by her absence.

I was serving as our ward's Relief Society president during this time, though my counselors had taken over for a few weeks before and after Mother's death. I felt no inclination to get back in the harness. A wise bishop, Kent Nelson, told me in a loving but firm way that it was time to serve again. He suggested I make a list of six women in the ward who needed a visit and resume my responsibilities. I hope those visits were helpful to *them*. I know for certain it was therapeutic for *me* to visit them. In a short time I was functioning again in my calling. Thinking of others had truly helped "the sun come up inside of me."

The Sun Comes Up inside of Me
Words and music by Janice Kapp Perry

I've heard it said and guess it's true, especially for the young
The thing that matters most in life is simply having fun

But good times last a moment, then they fade into the past
Where is the warm that lingers? Where is the joy that lasts?
So I look outside my circle for one who needs my help
And here's what happens every time I think of someone else

Chorus
    Oh, the sun comes up inside of me
    And a light goes on that helps me see
    That if I would be happy
    There's a price I must pay
    For all success is measured
    By the love we give away
    And the sun comes up inside of me
    And a light goes on that helps me see
    And it happens just like magic
    Each time I turn the key
    When I care about my brother
    Then the sun comes up inside of me

The one who wrote the rules of life is one who won't deceive
When He says there's joy in service, well, you really can believe
Your friends may think you're crazy and the world may call you fool
They may not see the power that's in the Golden Rule
But I've tried this way of living, I've put it to the test
And every time I help another, I am also blessed

Repeat Chorus

I've read it in the scriptures
And I've sung it in the hymns
I've learned that serving someone else
Is only serving Him
So I take Him at His promise
And I love the way it feels
That warm and welcome voice inside me
Saying this is real!

Repeat Chorus

Yes, the sun comes up inside of me

There Will Be Light

Toward the end of my term as ward Relief Society president I wrote and recorded an album of songs on very serious subjects. Musically treating the subjects of death, depression, loneliness, and sin was an interesting challenge.

I came to understand more fully that our hope in every difficult circumstance comes from having an unshakable faith and trust in our Savior, Jesus Christ. There are many times in life when we must walk by faith, looking forward to a future time when the eyes of our understanding will be opened and "there will be light."

The first song in this series came as a result of vicariously experiencing the depression of a few sisters in my acquaintance. Whether we experience the mild day-to-day depression that seems to affect us all occasionally or the truly debilitating depression experienced by a few, we must fight the battle to rise above these feelings, remembering that "God did not give us the spirit of fear, And if we take the first step He'll always be there, And there will be light." Counseling and medication are often necessary to break the cycle of acute, prolonged depression, but I have seen a deep faith and reliance upon God work miracles in some cases.

I hoped this recording would be not merely a collection of sad songs but rather a collection of songs of hope and comfort, filled with the conviction that His peace can be enough to sustain us through every trial.

There Will Be Light
Words and music by Janice Kapp Perry

I woke up this morning, I walked through the day
But the sun never seemed to come up
It's been quite a while now that things have seemed gray
They say I don't try hard enough
But the darkness seems heavy, the feeling so real
How can I rise again, when will I heal?
And then I remember, through sorrowful tears
God did not give me the spirit of fear
And if I take the first step, He'll always be there

Chorus
>   And there will be light, beautiful light
>   There will be light, sweet, saving light
>   Oh, it still won't be easy, I'll still have to fight
>   Just to see in the distance a small patch of white
>   Pulling me upward past blackness and night
>   Where there will be light

I can't quite explain how this emptiness feels
'Cause I don't understand it myself
But, friend, I can tell you, it hurts and it's real
And it feels like I'll never be well
If I say "I don't need you" or "leave me alone"
Never believe me, I'm lost on my own
Just help me remember that help is so near
God did not give me the spirit of fear
And if I take the first step, He'll always be there

Repeat Chorus

❖   ❖   ❖

There Is a Way Back

"There Is a Way Back" was part of my album of songs treating the subjects of depression, loneliness, death, and sin. Although most of us *want* to do what is right, the adversary can sometimes make black appear white, and with a few wrong choices, we can find ourselves in a downward spiral from which it is very difficult to recover. Often we feel we have gone too far and things are hopeless.

The words of the scriptures and of prophets assure us, however, that there is a way back. Because none of us has reached perfection, we are all in need of the saving power of Christ throughout our lives. Through the Atonement He has provided a way back when we have strayed.

The words and phrases of the scriptures are often very poetic and I especially love these comforting words from Isaiah: "Though your sins be as scarlet, they may be as white as snow; though they be red as crimson, they may be as wool."

One of the sweetest things I have ever witnessed is seeing a person who is deeply involved in sin decide to repent and accept the gift of the Atonement. It is so comforting to know there is a way back—*He* is the way.

There Is a Way Back

Words and music by Janice Kapp Perry

I want to win and I try so hard
Desire for sin was never in my heart
But at times I hear a whisper
Saying, "Once would be all right"
And I give in to the other side
And when you fall, it can be so hard
You taste the gall, you feel a broken heart
For the one who has deceived you
Making black appear as white
Can lead you down to an endless night

Chorus
 But there's a way back to where you were
 There is a way back, and the path is sure
 Because the Father's own Begotten Son
 Came to pay the price for all the wrong we've done
 Oh, He gave His life my soul to save
 Yes, the Son went down to the grave

There is a way, there is always light
There is a way, do not give up the fight
Though your sins may be as scarlet
They may be as white as snow
Just thank the Lord that He loves you so

Repeat Chorus

Though your sins be as scarlet
They may be as white as snow
Though they be red as crimson
They may be as white as wool

 There is a way back to where you were
 There is a way back, and the path is sure
 Because the Father's own Begotten Son
 Came to pay the price for all the wrong we've done

Oh, He gave His life my soul to save
Yes, the Son rose up from the grave

There is a way, He is the way

❖ ❖ ❖

In the Arms of His Love

In 1990 I received a call from Arizona author Steven A.
Cramer, who was preparing for the publication of a new book
entitled *In the Arms of His Love.* I was happy to make his
acquaintance, as I had enjoyed his previous books, *The Worth
of a Soul* and *Great Shall Be Your Joy.*

Brother Cramer, writing from the point of view of one who
had stood on the brink of despair because of his involvement
in serious sin and was rescued by the Savior, has helped many
to feel the love of the Savior and the implications of the Atonement in their lives. His new book was to be based on the comforting scripture "be faithful and diligent in keeping the commandments of God and I will encircle thee in the arms of my
love" (D&C 6:20). I have always loved that passage and had
often considered writing on that subject. Brother Cramer, realizing the power of music in helping us to internalize a principle, requested that I write a song entitled "In the Arms of His
Love" that would coincide with the release of his new book and
help provide an introduction to it.

I was pleased to have a reason to focus on that scripture. I
finished the song, and it was performed at a fireside in Salt Lake
City, where Brother Cramer was introducing his book by the
same title. It is the ultimate comfort to know that in the times
of our most difficult trials we may find safety, peace, and healing in the arms of His love.

In the Arms of His Love
Words and music by Janice Kapp Perry

There is but One who bore all things for us
There is but One who offers perfect love
Whatever earthly pain we know

He has descended far below
There is no sorrow He cannot comprehend
There is no suff'ring He cannot understand
He was forsaken, left alone
Our deepest pain to Him is known

Refrain
   In the arms of His love there is healing
   In the arms of His love there is hope
   There is One who is just
   There is One we can trust
   We are safe in the arms of His love

There is but One who brings eternal life
His yoke is easy and His burden light
Because He paid the price for sin
We may repent and come to Him
When we have wandered into the lonely night
He gently bids us return into the light
And when we fall and faith grows dim
There is forgiveness there with Him

Refrain
   In the arms of His love there is safety
   In the arms of His love there is peace
   There is One who is just
   There is One we can trust
   We are safe in the arms of His love

We are safe in the arms of His love

❖   ❖   ❖

Grandpa and Grandma Are Called On a Mission

My brother and sister-in-law Jack and Sue Kapp were called
to serve a mission in the Dominican Republic when they were
in their mid-fifties. That is a relatively young age for couples to
be called, so here is the rest of the story:

My brother graduated from Brigham Young University and
Utah State University, where he received bachelor's and master's

degrees in mechanical engineering. He then worked for thirty-five years as a structural design engineer, and at the time of his early retirement was director of engineering for Thiokol Chemical Corp. He was at the top of his career and well respected in his field.

He also suffered from arteriosclerosis and twice had undergone lifesaving heart by-pass surgeries. Feeling his mortality and having a great desire to serve a full-time mission with his wife, he made a life-changing decision to retire at the peak of his career. Out of curiosity one day I asked what it had cost him financially to retire ten years early and serve a mission. His conservative estimate was two million dollars.

After his retirement, Jack and Sue studied Spanish intensely for a year. When they received their call to the Dominican Republic, they accepted, knowing there would be no expert medical help available to them for eighteen months.

Jack and Sue had married at an early age, as had their children, so they had a sizable choir of grandchildren to sing at their farewell sacrament meeting. I thoroughly enjoyed writing a song that would help their grandchildren express their love and pride in their missionary grandparents.

Grandma and Grandpa Are Called on a Mission
Words and music by Janice Kapp Perry

Grandma and Grandpa, you're called on a mission
To spread the gospel light
You have the knowledge, the faith, and the wisdom
To testify of Christ

I'll miss your stories, your smiles, and your hugs
I'll miss the warmth of your special love
But when someone asks me, I'll answer with pride
"My Grandma and Grandpa are sharing the gospel of Jesus Christ"

Grandma and Grandpa, I see your example
And want to be like you
I will be learning and growing and earning
So I can serve Him too

I will be watching the things that you do
I will be praying each day for you

And when someone asks me, I'll answer with pride
"My Grandma and Grandpa are sharing the gospel of Jesus Christ"

❖ ❖ ❖

The Church of Jesus Christ

I am often asked if music comes to me when I'm sleeping and I have to get up and write it down. The answer is—rarely. I sleep quite soundly! This song, however, happened something like that.

I was taking a little cat nap in my studio one afternoon and awakened suddenly with the strong impression that there should be a song in the new Primary songbook containing the full name of our Church. Thus every child would become familiar with the name at a very early age. I knew the music for the new book had already been selected, but the feeling persisted, so I began by writing the full name of the Church in the first line.

Over two hours' time I dozed, awakened, and added lines several different times until I had written a full, two-verse song. I wrote the music that same day and sent it to Sister Pat Graham, who was supervising the production of the songbook. She responded favorably but said they would like to suggest a few changes in the words. As they made suggestions, they gave *me* the opportunity to make the adjustments. In the end, the song had just *one* verse and the only line that remained exactly intact from my "inspired" first effort was "I belong to The Church of Jesus Christ of Latter-day Saints!" Their ideas were excellent, and I contented myself with the thought that at least the idea to *have* such a song was inspired!

A year or two later I was delighted to hear little Junior Primary children in my ward singing the name of the Church confidently on the Primary sacrament meeting program. I wrote counterpoint words and melody for this song when we recorded it on a children's album entitled *The Church of Jesus Christ*.

The Church of Jesus Christ
Words and music by Janice Kapp Perry

Part One

    I belong to The Church of Jesus Christ of Latter-day Saints
    I know who I am, I know God's plan
    I'll follow Him in faith
    I believe in the Savior Jesus Christ
    I'll honor His name, I'll do what is right
    I'll follow His light
    His truth I will proclaim

Part Two

    This is the Church of Jesus Christ
    And it stands for good and truth and right
    I will follow His teachings
    Honor His dear name
    I will love Him, serve Him
    His truth proclaim

Both Parts Together

I'll do what is right
I'll follow His light
His truth I will proclaim

❖   ❖   ❖

The Voice of the Spirit

How we would love to see God's face or hear His voice, but for now, a veil separates us from His presence. Nevertheless, He does not leave us completely alone, for we feel His guidance through the still, small voice of the Spirit that speaks gently from deep inside us when we are worthy and when we are listening.

I have spent much of my life trying to identify and recognize the voice of the Spirit that gives guidance to our lives. Occasionally people in my acquaintance have said, matter-of-factly: "I prayed, and the Spirit said I should . . ." or "The Lord told me I should not . . ." While I admired *their* ability to hear the

Spirit's promptings so clearly, I wondered why they were not always that distinct for me. I had no doubt that I had been guided and even protected by spiritual promptings through my life, but oh how subtle they were—"a gentle voice so still and small, a voice that hardly can be heard at all."

When I was between the ages of about fifty and fifty-five, however, the Spirit spoke to me with such clarity on three occasions that there could be no doubt about the source of my enlightenment. All three of these experiences with the Spirit came while I was praying with real intent and felt in tune with the Lord. At none of these times did I expect such a direct answer to my prayers. It was at once exhilarating and comforting. The words seemed to be imprinted somehow in my mind. I would have to say I *felt* more than *heard* them, yet I am not sure. "The voice of the Spirit is so real to me, truth is revealed to me in heart and mind."

The Voice of the Spirit
Words and music by Janice Kapp Perry

Oh, God, my Eternal Father,
I long to see Thy face
But a veil was drawn between us
That I might live by faith
And yet I'm very certain
I do not walk alone
For when I seek Thee humbly
Thy wisdom is made known

Chorus
    The voice of the Spirit comes so quietly
    From deep inside of me to speak Thy will
    The voice of the Spirit comes as light to me
    Gently reminding me of all that's real
    A gentle voice, so still, so small
    A voice that hardly can be heard at all
    A voice so clear to me
    A voice that pierces me to my soul

Oh, God, my Eternal Father,
I love to hear Thy voice

But I left Thy loving presence
And came to earth by choice
And yet I feel Thy guidance
Each time I kneel to pray
Thy kind and caring Spirit
Illuminates my way

Chorus
> The voice of the Spirit is so sweet to me
> It whispers peace to me through thoughts divine
> The voice of the Spirit is so real to me
> Truth is revealed to me in heart and mind
> A gentle voice, so still, so small
> A voice that hardly can be heard at all
> A voice so clear to me
> A voice that pierces me to my soul

The voice of the Spirit is so sweet to me
A voice that teaches me all Thou would have me know

❖   ❖   ❖

When Jesus Comes Again

As a child I felt so sad whenever I heard the story of Jesus'
crucifixion and even felt some anger that wicked men had killed
Him before *I* had a chance to know Him (as a six-year-old, I
assumed Jesus should have lived forever). Mother explained
that it was all part of God's plan and that it wasn't final—Jesus
had been resurrected and would return to earth again.

Through my childhood I also learned of some terrible things
that would happen before He returned. I expressed my fears
about these things to my mother. She reassured me that if we
are prepared for His second coming we need not fear—it will
be a time of rejoicing for the faithful.

Decades later, as I watched my grandchildren coming into
the world, I wanted to write a song that would help them
understand and prepare for the Second Coming with a feeling
of joy.

When Jesus Comes Again
Words and music by Janice Kapp Perry

Jesus loved the little children
Taught and blessed each one of them
Then He left them with the promise
He would come again

No one knows the day or hour
When our Savior will appear
But we see the signs and wonders
Telling us the time is near

Chorus
    I am waiting, watching, praying
    Trying to be more like Him
    I will stand with faithful Saints
    When Jesus comes again
    When Jesus comes again

Jesus loves the little children
When He comes we need not fear
If we're ready, we'll be happy
When that day is here

He will come as light of morning
Shining brightly from the east
All the world will know Him then
And worship Him as Jesus Christ

Repeat Chorus

❖ ❖ ❖

Remember the Children

Third Nephi should be required reading for every person
who has ever abused a child in any way. Jesus commanded the
gathered crowd to bring the children to Him, and then He took
them one by one and blessed them. The occasion was so significant and beautiful that angels encircled them with fire from
heaven. Then Jesus spoke again, saying, "Behold your little

ones." Each one was blessed, and Jesus wept, sealing in our hearts forever a knowledge of the tender, loving regard He has for innocent children.

When a stake Primary president called and asked me to write a theme song for a regional conference, I was delighted. When she told me the theme was "Remember the Children," my heart nearly broke at receiving such a tender assignment. The theme was on my mind day and night until it was completed.

Our Savior admonished us to love, teach, and protect our little ones, yet our world today provides many distractions from our focus on home and family. How do we "remember" the children? We remember to give them love, to build their confidence, to lift them up in spirit, to teach them the gospel, to hold them and heal them and protect them from the evils of this world. We must love them as He did and teach them to trust in Him and watch for the day when He will come again.

When this song was recorded on one of our albums, it was sung by one of the kindest men I know, Dr. Thomas Myers, and his wife, Marilou. I considered it serendipitous that they also happened to have beautiful singing voices.

Remember the Children
Words and music by Janice Kapp Perry

Jesus commanded them to bring the children
He took them one by one and gently blessed them
Angels encircled them with fire from heaven
Then Jesus spoke again: "Behold your little ones."
Each one was blessed, and Jesus wept

Refrain
Remember the children
Remember to give them love
Remember to build them
Remember to lift them up
Remember to teach them
Of plain and precious things
Hold them and heal them
Comfort and shield them
Remember the children

Jesus commanded us to love the children
And He will stand with us if hearts are willing
Then, when the world's acclaim would pull us from them
We'll hear His voice again: "Behold your little ones."
Each one still bright with heaven's light

Repeat Refrain

Love them as He did then
Teach them to trust in Him
Until He comes again
Remember the children

❖   ❖   ❖

The Woman You'll Be Someday

In 1990 my mother, Ruth Kapp, was diagnosed with bone cancer and given perhaps a year to live. She had been a widow for twenty-one years and looked forward to the time she would be with Dad again, so her response was, "Well, doctor, I have my ticket home, don't I?" He returned a surprised smile and said honestly, "Yes, you do."

It was a difficult year as we watched Mother go from crutches, to a walker, to a wheelchair, and finally to bed as a result of various surgeries and treatments. Still, she maintained a certain optimism and excitement about her impending "graduation from mortality" that I admired and even envied.

During one of the trying nights of her illness, she pushed the buzzer that would bring me from the adjoining bedroom to assist her. She felt strange and just wanted company. I lay down on the bed beside her, held her hand, and asked, "Mother, how can you be at the end of your life, having gone through so much this year, and yet you are peaceful and even happy at the prospect of taking the next step? I want to feel as you do when I reach that time."

In answer, she reviewed her life and realized her peace of mind came from having made correct decisions all through her life. She married a good man at the right time and in the right place, she stayed home with her children, she developed talents to a high degree, and she gave willing Church service.

After Dad died at a young age (fifty-seven) she served a full-time mission in Jackson, Mississippi. When she returned she devoted her time to genealogical pursuits, researching and entering more than forty thousand names for temple work. She gave great service to her family, neighbors, and people she had brought into the Church. In short, she had kept her second estate and was ready in every way for the next step.

Mother shared a poem with me that she had written thirty years earlier for a speech she was giving to the young women in her stake. It is a lengthy poem, so I'll share just a few lines:

You—Grown Old

There's a little old woman up there ahead
Who somehow resembles you
She has your nose, your chin, your eyes—
She walks and talks like you too.

Whether she loves or despises you
Is all up to you I am told
You brought her gladness or sadness
For you see, she is you, grown old.

–Ruth S. Kapp

The poem answered my question perfectly and was my mother's last message to me. I loved her idea and asked, "May I take your idea, add some thoughts of my own, and write a song on that subject?"

"Well, that depends," she said with a twinkle in her eye. "Will you pay me royalties?" I promised I would, if she would leave her forwarding address.

I entitled my version of our song "The Woman You'll Be Someday," and played and sang it for her before she died. We recorded the song on an album the very morning she died, and we played it softly in her room that evening as we waited for the funeral home to come for her.

We send her royalties to a woman who is continuing Mother's genealogical research.

The Woman You'll Be Someday
Words and music by Janice Kapp Perry

I see an old woman rocking there
The sun shining softly on her silver hair
I wonder the secrets she holds deep inside
Is she smiling or hiding a tear in her eye?
She watches our day as her story unfolds
For you see, she is you, grown old
And with every decision you make today
You're creating the woman you'll be someday
Just for now the old woman depends on you
She waits and she watches
As you make her dreams come true

Be kind to the woman waiting there
For time passes swiftly, and you must prepare
Hold fast to the values more precious than gold
And you'll bless the old woman who waits down the road
She watches our day as her story unfolds
For you see, she is you, grown old
Only you have the power to make her whole
Only you can decide her eternal role
Just for now the old woman depends on you
She waits and she watches
As you make her dreams come true

Be watchful, young woman,
Choose well today!
Remember to live for
The woman you'll be someday

❖ ❖ ❖

As You Are Called to Serve

During my childhood and early years of marriage I rarely, if ever, heard of mature couples being called to full-time missionary service, except as the president of a mission. During the past decade, however, many have been called, and the Brethren are urging all who are able, to serve. In our travels throughout the United States on speaking assignments, we constantly hear mission presidents lauding the accomplishments of their faithful missionary couples and wishing they had many more such couples in their missions.

We visited my aunt and uncle Mervin and Rae Preston as they served in the Tampa Bay Florida Mission and could see they were on fire with the spirit of missionary work. Many in their small branch testified of the great difference they had made in the lives of the Saints there, particularly the less actives. Their maturity, gospel experience, and boundless love for others brought scores of people into Church activity.

We later visited our dear friends Kent and Sara Nelson while they were serving on the Big Island of Hawaii. They served their whole mission in an isolated small ward, baptizing many, activating others, and loving the people into greater activity. As their humble Bishop Cathcart said to us, "These two people alone came to our troubled ward and turned our hearts back to God."

It isn't easy to leave children and grandchildren and worldly comforts to serve full-time missions. But a lifetime of gospel living and leadership experience and learning the power of love can make a huge difference in the lives of many earnest, seeking people throughout the world who deserve to hear the gospel message.

I wrote this song for a retired couple who were leaving on a full-time mission. It is dedicated to all who have the courage to go.

As You Are Called to Serve
Words and music by Janice Kapp Perry

You bring a lifetime of love
You bring a lifetime of learning
And hearts that now are yearning to share the truths you know
You bring a lifetime of faith
You bring a lifetime of wisdom
From trials you've been given to help your spirits grow
You turn your hearts from home

And leave the ones you love
You go in perfect faith that God will bear you up

Refrain
    And now as you are called to serve
    To do His will, to share His sacred word
    He has promised angels will watch over you
    In this, His work, as you are called to serve

You bring a lifetime of hope
You bring a lifetime of giving
Of faithful gospel living, and standing for the right
You bring a lifetime of joy
You bring a lifetime of caring
Of quietly preparing, and now the field is white
And when your trials come
As you serve side by side
His pow'r will lift you up, His love in you abide

Repeat Refrain

He has promised angels will watch over you
In this, His work, as you are called to serve

❖   ❖   ❖

He Gives Me Strength

In 1992 I received a letter from a seventeen-year-old young woman named Liz Barson. When I opened the letter a picture fell out, a picture of a beautiful, dark-haired girl in a long-sleeved white dress. I vaguely noted her sweet expression and then began to read her letter.

Liz mentioned that she was often asked to speak at firesides and wondered if I would write a theme song for her programs. As I read on through the beautifully crafted penmanship in her letter, she told me more about herself and added, almost as an afterthought, that she was asked to speak because she had been born with no arms and had learned a few things she could share with others.

She definitely had my attention at that point. I picked up the picture again and saw what I had not noticed the first time—the long white sleeves hung limply from her shoulders.

My mind raced with a thousand questions as I tried to imagine living my life without arms or hands. How had she fixed her hair for the picture? How had she put her dress on? And buttoned or zipped it? How had she written the letter?

I answered her immediately, saying that I would be honored to write the song, but I needed to know and understand her feelings before I could do so. I asked her to write and describe how her life had been to help me to understand what should be in the song. Also, I said, please tell me how you wrote that letter!

After a short delay, her carefully penned answer arrived. She explained that she uses her toes to hold the pen to write and also to perform other daily tasks. But more than that, her letter revealed some of the hurt she had felt through her life from thoughtless children and the triumph she has felt as friends matured and realized her true worth. The solid thread running through every sentence of her letter was how she drew strength from her Savior, Jesus Christ, who had been hurt and hated more than she ever could be.

I was touched by her faith and positive attitude and felt privileged to write her song. I also resolved to quit complaining about a disability with my left hand—so minor compared to her challenges.

A few years after I wrote the song, I spoke at a chapel near Liz's home. She joined me that day, spoke briefly, and sang her song. She was a college student then, surrounded by great friends who came to hear her, and I marveled once more at her accomplishments and her great spirit.

He Gives Me Strength
Words and music by Janice Kapp Perry

He didn't give me everything
I might have needed to take me far
He didn't give me everything
I might have wanted to make me a star

If it were up to me
I might have chosen diff'rently
But then maybe not
For I have been taught
By what He withheld from me

Chorus
    He gives me strength to make it
    He heals my heart when others break it
    He's there for me
    He gives me strength to make it
    He who Himself was hurt and hated
    More than I could ever be
    He strengthens me

He didn't give me everything
No silver platter, no life of ease
He didn't give me everything
I might have needed to help me succeed
Yet in my heart I see
He knows what is best for me
So I will go on
And write my own song
With what He has given me

Repeat Chorus

I'll show my love for Him
I put my trust in Him
Running the race, walking by faith
Until I'm home again with Him

Repeat Chorus

❖   ❖   ❖

The Least of These

    I was serving as ward Relief Society president in Provo during the Relief Society's sesquicentennial celebration year. As part of the Church-wide celebration, each local Relief Society unit was encouraged to reach out beyond ward boundaries in on-going acts of service. Our ward decided to serve in a different area each month and acquaint ourselves with the different needs that existed in our area. Three places of service affected me deeply, and each was inspiration for one verse of the song "The Least of These."

1. A woman in our ward had been placed in a rest home by her children. I knew the decision had to be made, but I was disappointed to see that her family rarely visited her. We set up a schedule of regular visitors for this sweet sister. It was obvious that visitors brightened her life greatly. She added much to our lives also, for she still had many wonderful stories to share.

2. I had not even been aware of Provo's homeless shelter before our decision to serve there during this eye-opening year. Some say the homeless bring on their own problems and feel little sympathy for their plight, but as we prepared and served the food, talked with the homeless while they ate, and cleaned up afterward, we heard many stories of hardship and illness beyond their control that had brought them to this point of dependency. Two lines from the song express how I came to feel: "The measure of a life is what we share, How we care about God's hurting children everywhere."

3. The women's prison in Draper provided the third significant experience. We attended their Relief Society and provided craft materials from which they made Christmas presents for loved ones. Afterward we mailed the gifts to the addresses the inmates provided. We met with these women more than once, and except for their clothing I could tell no difference between their Relief Society and our own—same prayers, same songs, same lessons, same hopes and aspirations for their families. These were good women who had made serious mistakes. "The only thing that He expects of me is to willingly forgive as He's forgiven me, And bless my sister in her need."

Toward the end of His ministry, Jesus knelt and washed the feet of each disciple—an unmistakable message to us all to lose ourselves in the service of others. This year of service helped me to understand the joy that comes from service, and I wrote the song to help me remember those feelings.

The Least of These

Words and music by Janice Kapp Perry

I see her sitting all alone
In a white and sterile nursing home
Day after day she sits that way
Her eyelids droop and her shoulders stoop
It's not a life that she would choose
One lonely soul, a castaway
And she waits to hear the footsteps down the hall
Maybe this will be the day an old-time friend will call
She needs a kindly word, that's all

Chorus

    Lord, help me love the least of these
    Help me to go where Thy light leads me
    Give me a heart that sees another's need
    And love to share with the least of these

He hasn't much to call his own
And I know he makes the street his home
No one to fill his hungering
Though some may say in lofty tones
"He only reaps what he has sown"
We cannot know his suffering
And the measure of a life is what we share
How we care about God's hurting children everywhere
For they have burdens we could bear

Repeat Chorus

His life is sad for he is held
In a gray and lonely prison cell
Year after year, behind dark walls
Don't know his crime, but I know this much:
It's really not for me to judge
That's God's domain, as I recall
And the only thing that He expects of me
Is to willingly forgive as He's forgiven me
And bless my brother in his need

Repeat Chorus

For in their faces I believe that I can see
A chance for me to show my love for Thee

Repeat Chorus

And love to share with the least of these

❖   ❖   ❖

There Is Eternity

So many times in my life I have seen wonderful, faithful Saints blindsided by tragedies that threaten to undermine the very foundations of their faith: two beautiful daughters are killed by a drunken driver on their way to sing at a friend's missionary farewell; a beloved child leaves home to live a homosexual lifestyle and returns to his parents' home dying of AIDS; an Aaronic Priesthood holder becomes addicted to drugs and his promising life is wasted; one spouse in a covenant marriage learns that the other spouse has been unfaithful and is unrepentant; the parents of a teenager learn that their son has taken his own life.

I know people who have experienced these tragedies and many others and have observed their desperate struggle to find some meaning in what has happened that would bring them peace of mind and understanding. Some have lost their faith and been unable to recover spiritually. Some live the rest of their lives asking the futile question, "Why?" And some are spiritually strengthened by tragedy.

Some heartaches just can never be explained or understood, and for our lifetime we have to just hold on through all the hopelessness we feel, trusting that there is no earthly sorrow heaven cannot heal. We must keep the faith, trust in God's omniscient wisdom, and know that eternity is ahead in which we will receive healing in God's presence.

There Is Eternity
Words and music by Janice Kapp Perry

Trials come on any days, they come in unexpected ways
'Til sorrow seems more than the heart can hold
A broken dream, a loved one lost

Too deep the hurt, too high the cost
And questions stir within a troubled soul
But some heartaches just can never be explained
And no caring words can take away the pain
And just one saving thought remains

There is eternity to know the reason why
There is eternity for blessings now denied
There will our sorrows cease
There we'll find lasting peace
Just hold on through all the hopelessness you feel
There is no earthly sorrow heaven cannot heal

Trials come to everyone, from out of nowhere heartaches come
Where is the hand that heals and holds us up
A faithless love, a broken trust
A wound so painful, so unjust
And deep inside we cry "It is too much!"
But some heartaches just can never be explained
And no caring words can take away the pain
And just one saving thought remains

There is eternity to heal a broken heart
There is eternity where loved ones never part
There we will understand
The Father's loving plan
Just hold on through all the hopelessness you feel
There is no earthly sorrow heaven cannot heal

When hurt confuses me, my faith renews in me
One quiet thought that soothes my soul and carries me:
The Father knows my need
He answers when I plead,
"There is eternity."

❖ ❖ ❖

Where Earth and Heaven Meet

I have written several songs about the temple, but this one was from a little different perspective. I wrote this piece on a day when I had gone to the temple to find peace and inspiration for my life. In the lyrics I tried to recall the feelings and impressions I had had from the moment I entered the doors of the Provo temple that day until I left two hours later to return home.

It seems that no matter what else is happening in my life, when I walk through the doors of the temple I feel a tangible lightening of my earthly burdens and concerns. Sitting with my brothers and sisters dressed in simple white, I perceive that we are all equal in God's sight and are collectively striving to draw near to Him through our temple service.

I love to renew the sacred covenants I have made with the Lord; I love to be reminded of the big picture when I am struggling with the pressing cares of the day; I love the sense of connection I feel with beloved ancestors who have paved the way for my present happiness; and I love just to sit quietly and reflect and pray for guidance and inspiration.

It is always with reluctance that I leave the temple and return to the pressures of everyday life, but I always feel better prepared to meet the challenges after I have felt the renewing spirit there.

Where Earth and Heaven Meet

Words and music by Janice Kapp Perry

I enter quietly, I hear the closing of the door
My heart stirs silently, I'm in the world no more
The perfect beauty here invites all Saints who qualify
To leave all earthly cares behind and come to Christ
Each dressed in simple white
All equal in God's sight
Life's purposes unfold before my eyes

As Spirit teaches me I feel a quiet peace
Here in this holy house where earth and heaven meet

I listen willingly, renewed once more in faith and love
Each saving ordinance revealed by God above
With every covenant I make my soul is sanctified
As I am then endowed with power from on high
Each promised blessing here

Is sealed by priesthood power
And I am richly blessed this sacred hour

I witness once for self and then for others speak
Here in this holy house where earth and heaven meet

I leave reluctantly, I hear the closing of the door
My heart stirs silently, I'm in the world once more
Life's sweetest blessings sealed, God's will for me revealed
His love my protection and my shield
My purpose clearer, life's meaning more complete
Here in this holy house where earth and heaven meet

Here in this holy house where earth and heaven meet

❖   ❖   ❖

Be of Good Cheer

In 1990 the leaders of Lambda Delta Sigma asked me to write a song on the subject of their guiding principle, "Be of Good Cheer." I had written a song for them years earlier and had gained great respect and admiration for the goals of their organization. I was very pleased to work with them again.

It is so common for women of all ages to become tired, overwhelmed, and discouraged to the point that they scarcely notice the beautiful and positive things that are all around them daily. This song is a plea to the Lord to help us have eyes to see, ears to hear, and hearts to feel all that He has blessed us with—to help us overcome fears and have an awareness of our own divinity.

This song was written during a very difficult time in my own life, and it helped me greatly in my quest to retrain my mind and heart to be of good cheer.

Be of Good Cheer
Words and music by Janice Kapp Perry

Lord, give me eyes to see the wonders of this earth
Help me to only seek the things of greatest worth

Bless me through sun and rain to feel that Thou art near
To put my trust in Thee and be of good cheer
Lord, give me ears to hear the music of my soul—
The song of redeeming love I learned so long ago
Help me to always sense my own divinity
To rise above my fears and be of good cheer
I feel thy hand in nature's beauty, feel thy perfect love for me
And I'll be strong because I may depend on saving help from Thee

Lord, help me show my thanks to those who love me best
Knowing they strengthen me for ev'ry earthly test
Fill me with gratitude for all that I hold dear
Help me to cherish life and be of good cheer
Help me, when trials come, to see beyond the pain
To clear skies and sunny days when I'll feel peace again
Help me to walk with Thee in faith through all my days
Learning to dry my tears and be of good cheer
The Spirit testifies I knew Thee before the world was
And though a veil was drawn, I still recall the power of Thy love

Lord help me know that Thou wilt lift me when I fall
Help me to understand that Thou art over all
Give me a happy heart with vision bright and clear
Bless me and lift me up
Help me to feel thy love
And be of good cheer

❖   ❖   ❖

Born of Water, Born of Spirit

Nearly a decade ago my husband and I were involved with
a dear friend and faithful Church member who had committed
serious transgression and was brought before a Church disci-
plinary council. He spoke before the council in humility,
expressing deep sorrow for his sin and a willingness to accept
the censure of his brethren and the Lord.

The council resulted in his excommunication from the Church
for an undetermined length of time. Those presiding explained

to him that the Spirit of the Holy Ghost would withdraw for a season and he would be left to struggle on his own. We watched as our friend suffered the humility of informing his family members and friends and asking for their understanding and support.

The ensuing year was a devastating experience as he was necessarily brought to the point of feeling godly sorrow for his sins. Only through frequent priesthood blessings from a faithful home teacher and bishop was he able to overcome the power of darkness that frequently settled over him and his family.

To his great credit, he never wavered from his desire to return to the light and full fellowship in the Church. A new man emerged from this significant experience, one who had been healed of any desire for sin and who felt worthy once again to be in full fellowship with the Saints. The Lord confirmed this feeling in the heart and mind of the stake president, and a date for his baptism was scheduled.

I wrote this song for the occasion, and his family performed it at the service. The line that now reads "My heart is turning to the light" originally said "I am returning to the light." It was changed so that the piece may be used at any baptism.

Born of Water, Born of Spirit

Words and music by Janice Kapp Perry

Today I stand at water's edge
Today with humble heart I pledge
I will be buried with Thee, Lord,
I will enter at the door
Rising to a life divinely new

Today with hands upon my head
By priesthood pow'r I will be blessed
Lord, send thy Spirit from above
From the fountains of thy love
Bless me now as I begin anew

May the water now surround and make me whole
Wash away my past and cleanse my willing soul
Let the Holy Ghost descending like a dove
Bear witness of Thy sweet redeeming love

Chorus
>   Born of water, born of Spirit
>   Renewed in faith and covenant with Thee
>   Born of water, born of Spirit
>   By love's atoning sacrifice made free
>   With my spirit now refined
>   Heart and soul to thee inclined
>   Born of water, born of Spirit
>   Child of Thine

Today I come in simple white
My spirit willing and contrite
Please bless and fill me with Thy peace
Let my faith in Thee increase
Knowing in Thy love I will be safe

Today with spirit burning bright
My heart is turning to the light
Thy sweetest blessings I desire
Touch me now with heaven's fire
Let thy Spirit sanctify this day

May the water now surround and make me whole
Wash away my past and cleanse my willing soul
Let the Holy Ghost descending like a dove
Bear witness of Thy sweet redeeming love

Chorus
>   Born of water, born of Spirit
>   Renewed in faith and covenant with Thee
>   Born of water, born of Spirit
>   By love's atoning sacrifice made free
>   Lord, to Thee, my heart is known
>   Please receive me as Thine own
>   Born of water, born of Spirit
>   Born of water, born of Spirit
>   Turning home

❖   ❖   ❖

Like Jesus

On my morning walk around the Provo temple I often pass Brother Reed Benson, son of Ezra Taft Benson, going the opposite direction. He always responds with a tip of his hat and a cheery greeting as he passes, making me smile every time. One morning he reversed his route, walked with me for about a block, and asked if he could stop by our house to get a copy of the *I Walk by Faith* CD for his teenaged daughter.

He came the next day, and after a short visit I gave him the CD. When I refused payment, he said, "I'll be back." The next day he came by to give me the book *In His Steps* by Charles W. Sheldon. Brother Benson is a religion professor at BYU and gives extra credit to those in his classes who will read this book. "Let me know how you feel about it when you've finished," he said.

I began reading that very day and kept going until I finished. The book told the story of a midwestern Protestant minister who made a contract with God that in every circumstance of his life, large or small, he would ask himself, "What would Jesus do?" and then act accordingly, regardless of the consequences. He eventually persuaded many in his congregation to make a similar contract, and the book chronicles their various experiences of devastating financial loss, persecution, and derision as they followed this course. Ultimately, we see the great inner peace and calm that come into their lives as they become truly Christlike in every aspect of their lives.

I loved the book and knew while I was reading it that my response would come in the form of a song—my way of internalizing something I have learned. When the song was written, I recorded and presented a copy to Brother Benson with gratitude for his meaningful gift. I have sung this piece at the conclusion of my programs for years.

Like Jesus
Words and music by Janice Kapp Perry

I want to be like Jesus, I want to see as He sees
I want to look into the hearts of others

And see the best that they can be
I want to be like Jesus, I want to feel what He feels
I want to be a person of compassion
And always speak the word that heals

Chorus
> And so I'll try in every situation
> To let His light come shining through
> When I'm unsure I'll ask myself this question:
> "What would Jesus do?"

I want to be like Jesus, I want to love as He loves
And when I see someone in need of kindness
I want to care the way He does
I want to be like Jesus, I want to give as He gives
I want to try to live my life for others
And to forgive as He forgives

Repeat Chorus

He is divine, my Savior, my Redeemer
And I still walk imperfectly
But I can live so all the world will notice
A little bit of Jesus in me

❖ ❖ ❖

No Greater Work

Just before my husband fell asleep one night in 1993, I nudged him and whispered, "Honey, I need a song idea for the *Ensign* songwriting contest—the deadline is just a few days away. *Please!*" In a sleepy voice he whispered, "No greater work." "That's nice," I said, "but what does it mean?" With his last ounce of consciousness he answered, "President McKay said there is no greater work than that which we do within the walls of our own homes—now goodnight, honey."

Then he slept away. But his idea intrigued me so much I had to get out of bed and start working on it even though it was midnight.

This was a subject I truly believed in. During graduate school I needed to provide income for our family so Doug could concentrate on his studies. I could not bear to leave our three (and then four) little ones in someone else's care, so I baby-sat other children and did typing for students and professors in our little apartment after the children were in bed. We wanted our children to learn *our* values, and that required our being with them through the experiences of each day. And how I would hate to have missed all the unforgettably sweet and challenging experiences I shared with them each day.

I have never had a desire to be anywhere but in our home. Writing this song let me give expression to some of my deeply held feelings on this subject. It had success in the contest—and I shared the prize money with Doug, of course!

No Greater Work
Words and music by Janice Kapp Perry

This is my home, my haven from the world
Where little children watch in perfect trust
They hear my words, they see the things I do
And in my kind and gentle care
They learn to love

Chorus
> This is my home
> My heaven here on earth
> And in my home I find
> The things of greatest worth
> This is my home
> And here I'll gladly serve
> For in my heart I know
> There is no greater work

This is my home, my refuge from the storm
Where my companion waits to comfort me
I offer strength and caring in return
I give eternal love and pure fidelity

Repeat Chorus

This is my home, a place that I will share
A place for all who need my love and care

And as I help each stranger in my way
I know the Savior's loving Spirit will be there

Repeat Chorus

No greater work than this
No sweeter place to serve
And in my heart I know
There is no greater work

❖   ❖   ❖

Stand Up, Walk Away

All that we read, see, listen to, watch, or otherwise take into our minds becomes a part of us—it's who we are. The subconscious mind can store an infinite number of sounds and images that are there for later recall. Elder Russell M. Nelson has said: "Our bodies have been created to accommodate our spirits, to allow us to experience the challenges of mortality. . . . With this understanding, it is pure sacrilege to let anything enter the body that might defile the physical temple of God. It is irreverent to let even the gaze of our precious eyesight, or the sensors of our touch or hearing, supply the brain with memories that are unclean or unworthy" (*The Power within Us* [Salt Lake City: Deseret Book, 1988], 11).

This song, which supports the section on media in the booklet *For the Strength of Youth,* urges the youth of the Church to listen to the still, small voice that warns them when something is not appropriate and to have the courage to "stand up and walk away" from that situation without hesitation. The conclusion urges them to fill their minds with all the best and simply shut out all the rest.

Stand Up, Walk Away
Words and music by Janice Kapp Perry

Whatever you read, whatever you listen to
Whatever you see will make an impression on you

Whatever you watch, whatever you take into your mind
You'll find it is true, whatever you view becomes you
So if you don't think it's appropriate
Don't see it, don't read it, don't participate
Just have the courage to

Chorus
    Stand up, walk away
    Change the channel, refuse to stay
    Close the cover or throw it away
    Have the courage to lead the way

Whenever you sense that something's not right for you
Don't ever pretend that it is all right to do
Whenever you hear a quiet voice warning you to go
Get up and be gone. You've got to be strong when it's wrong
And you might give in if you hesitate
Don't do it, don't view it, it's a big mistake
Just have the courage to

Repeat Chorus

The world is full of wonderful scenes
So seek for good and beautiful things
Fill your mind with all the best
And simply shut out all the rest
Just have the courage to

Repeat Chorus

Stand up, walk away

❖   ❖   ❖

There Is a Power in Music

Music has the power to move us, teach us, and touch us spiritually. The words, the music, and the rhythm combine to have a powerful effect on us. Unfortunately, when God creates something good and beautiful, Satan creates a counterfeit. That is true in almost every aspect of our lives, and particularly, I believe, in the area of music.

In 1993, Joy Lundberg and I collaborated on an album of songs in support of the Church's booklet for youth, *For the Strength of Youth*. One of the songs for which I wrote both words and music was titled "There Is a Power in Music." In 1999 I spoke to a youth group in Maryland and sang this song. A mother of one of the youth related the following story the next day in testimony meeting.

She had insisted that her reluctant teenaged son attend our program, and she came with him. Just before we began, he retreated to the foyer, and she assumed her efforts had been for nothing. She stayed, however, and afterward they drove home in silence. Without a word the boy went directly to their media room, gathered up inappropriate videos and CDs, and put them in a box. He then placed all their Church videos and CDs and those by LDS writers on the shelves by the TV and sound system, announcing to his mom that he was going to listen only to good music and watch good videos from now until his mission (this was his first mention of a mission!).

Perhaps it was the song that touched him, or maybe it was the story I had related. A friend told me about her son who had always been a good boy making good choices, except for listening to heavy metal music. He continued on this course and had now been on his mission for several months. But recently he wrote home to his younger brother and described what a difficult time he had had ridding his mind of the inappropriate words and music that were there. Finally, after fasting and prayer and a blessing from his mission president, he was free of it and could better proceed with his missionary work. He was writing to plead with his younger brother to make a better choice of music than he had. There is, indeed, a power in music.

There Is a Power in Music
Words and music by Janice Kapp Perry

There's a magic in music
That reaches my soul
Something catchy in music

That seems to take control
When the music is soft and sacred
It feels just like a prayer
But when the music gets wild and crazy
It's then I must beware

Chorus
   There is a power in music
   And I want to use it to receive the light
   There is a power in music
   And I must refuse it when it isn't right

There's a magic in music
A touch of romance
Something happens in music
That makes me want to dance
When the music is light and lovely
It lifts me up so high.
When the music is sad and lonely
It makes me want to cry

Repeat Chorus

There's a magic in music
That goes to my head
There's a passion in music
That words cannot express
When the music is sweet it soothes me
And puts my heart at rest
When the music is bold it moves me
With charm that can possess

Repeat Chorus

There's a magic in music
That comes from above
Something there in the music
That helps me feel God's love

❖   ❖   ❖

I Will Remember Thee

The words of the sacrament prayer, according to the Prophet Joseph Smith, were "obtained of Him [Jesus Christ] . . . by the spirit of prophecy and revelation." No wonder we love the words of that prayer so much! In partaking of the sacrament we witness to God our willingness to take upon us the name of Jesus Christ and always remember Him and keep His commandments.

After a marvelous trip to Israel with BYU Travel Study in 1989, I wrote a sacred cantata entitled *Remember Me* that attempted to convey the spirit of all I had felt and experienced there. In one of the pieces, "I Will Remember Thee," I enumerated several specific times when we witness that we remember our Savior—at the time of our baptism, when we partake of the sacrament each week, when we make covenants in the temple, and when we pray to the Father in His name. We further remember Him by keeping His commandments, forgiving and helping others, repenting, and showing Christlike love toward others. Our hearts and minds should always be filled with His Spirit, and our actions will show we remember Him.

When the sacrament prayer is spoken humbly and from the heart by our young priests, it is a special gift to those who will partake. I recall one singular experience concerning the sacrament prayer. Doug and I were asked to speak and sing in an all-black LDS ward in High Point, North Carolina, several years ago. Two distinguished black men in their fifties spoke the words of the sacrament prayer with such humility, tenderness, and devotion that I could not resist opening my eyes briefly to see if the Savior was there with them. It is truly a highlight of each week to renew at the sacrament table this heartfelt promise: I will remember Thee.

I Will Remember Thee
Words and music by Janice Kapp Perry

Dear Savior, I have witnessed
At water's edge, my humble pledge:

I will remember Thee
Dear Savior, I have witnessed
With broken bread and cup afresh
I will remember Thee

By each commandment I obey
By helping others on their way
I will remember Thee
By every trespass I forgive
By every loving word I give
I will remember Thee
Remember Thee

Dear Savior, I have witnessed
In temple white, I'll seek Thy light
I will remember Thee
Dear Savior, I have witnessed
On bended knee, Thy love for me
I will remember Thee

By every fervent prayer I speak
By every covenant I keep
I will remember Thee
By every miracle I see
By every act of charity
I will remember Thee
Remember Thee

I will eat of the bread
I will drink from the cup, worthily
By thy word I'll be fed
By thy light I'll be led, willingly
I will share the love
That Thou hast given me
I will remember
I will remember Thee

❖   ❖   ❖

Surround Yourself with Joy

In 1994, a stake Relief Society president from California said to me, "We would like you to speak on our theme, 'Surround Yourself with Joy.'" I agreed, but after I hung up the phone I felt puzzled about the meaning of the phrase. The next day I left for our cabin to ponder this intriguing idea and to try to write a song that would help me understand it.

How wonderful it would be if we could just choose to have joyful, happy experiences every day. Unfortunately, that would not provide a very conclusive test for this probationary period of our existence. The reality is that life holds much sorrow for each of us, often from circumstances over which we have little or no control. On the other hand, we each have relatively calm periods (between trials), and that's when we need to set aside the memories of the difficult times and choose to experience some genuine joy.

The lyrics describe a few of the things that bring me great joy. When I can choose, I love to surround myself with children (my grandchildren), good and caring friends and family, soothing and uplifting music, beautiful scenes of nature, silence and solitude, and anything peaceful that helps me feel the love of God.

I loved pondering this subject. I sent the song ahead to the stake where I was to speak, and it was introduced by a lovely Relief Society chorus that morning. Since then, I am much more aware of times when I can actually choose to surround myself with joy.

Surround Yourself with Joy
Words and music by Janice Kapp Perry

Chorus
 Life holds much of sorrow
 That we cannot avoid
 So when you have the chance
 When you have the choice
 Surround yourself with joy

Surround yourself with children
So innocent and sweet

For life can seem so simple
If you can make believe
Surround yourself with music
And you'll find solace there
For when your heart is tender
Your song becomes a prayer

Repeat Chorus

Surround yourself with friendship
When you feel all alone
For in the love of others
The sweetest joys are known
Surround yourself with beauty
Enjoy God's handiwork
In sights and sounds of nature
The voice of God is heard.

Repeat Chorus

Surround yourself with silence
For when you are alone
The whis'prings of the Spirit
Are quietly made known
Surround yourself with heaven
In every waking thought
For there is peace and safety
Within the love of God

Repeat Chorus

> When you have the chance
> When you have the choice
> Surround yourself with joy

❖   ❖   ❖

Couples

Over the years I've tried many times to write a special love
song for my husband. I take notes, but when I can't get it
"just right," I set it aside for a future day. I suppose the song

I want to write is a bit lofty and thus elusive. One day I decided just to write a realistic song about the give and take of marriage. It was written tongue-in-cheek, and yet it's oh so true! Whenever I perform it on our firesides, women will afterwards ask, "Where can I find a copy of these words—that's just how it is for us!"

Our relationship with our spouse requires a lifetime of attention. A healthy sense of humor can help a whole lot!

Couples
Words and music by Janice Kapp Perry

After thirty-six years I have learned quite a lot
About what things will please him and what things will not
So our marriage is blissfully calm and serene
Except for a few insignificant things:

In raising our children we certainly clicked
Except I'm too easy and he's much too strict
But a little of his way, a little of mine
And it seems that the kids have all grown up just fine

We both enjoy movies but know in advance
That he'll choose adventure and I'll choose romance
Yes, we do have a few little problems like these—
Like he says half his life is spent finding my keys

He loves his computers—he bought one for me
He wants me to learn it, but I won't agree
He'll talk about floppies and hardware and ROMS
When I don't even know how to turn the thing on!

When it comes to music, we're solid it seems
Except he loves classics, and country suits me
But in this decision we're compromised fairly—
No high-brow, no low-brow—just Janice Kapp Perry!

When it comes to TV we're exactly the same
We love basketball, football, all BYU games
But I prefer watching one game at a time
While he flips the channels to watch eight or nine

If I had the chance I would willingly choke
The guy who invented the remote!

We found a solution that works usually
His TV is upstairs, my downstairs, you see
But we are united each time our team scores—
I whistle and clap, and he stomps on the floor

I'm sure he's observed I'm a little too round
But he says he just loves me more by the pound
Then I can't resist pointing out lovingly
That while I gained thirty he gained forty-three

Just lately he's noticed my hair's turning gray
Then quickly pretends that he likes it that way
So I pat his bald spot and say with a flare:
"At least I am blessed with a full head of hair!"

Except for these few little things I have mentioned
Our marriage is really quite nearly perfection
We've had disagreements, but as I recall
We just did things his way—no problem at all!

He may see things differently—I could be wrong—
But I get the last word, cause I wrote the song!

❖ ❖ ❖

Far Different Places

A woman in Oregon spoke to me after a musical fireside presentation and asked if I would consider writing a song for families, like hers, who have children with Down syndrome. In thinking about it later I realized I had had several such requests just in the past few months. This focused me on the *need* for such music, but I felt unqualified to write about what I had not experienced myself. I approached my cousin Joy Lundberg (who had had first-hand experience in rearing children with disabilities) about writing most of the lyrics for an album on this subject. She did so in a very personal and masterful way.

Still, I personally wanted to understand what it is like dealing with disabilities in a family on a daily basis, so I interviewed twenty mothers whose children had Down syndrome or other disabilities, sometimes asking them to put their feelings in writing. This was a period of intense learning for me, and one of the most touching experiences I have ever been involved in. From their tender responses I fashioned words for the song "Far Different Places," a story that begins in the hospital as parents first learn their child has Down syndrome (or other problems), and progresses through their adjustment as their life's journey takes them "to far different places than [they] had ever dreamed."

My very thick file of pictures, letters, and stories on this subject is a treasure to me, and I occasionally reread them just to gain perspective. The mother who originally requested the song wrote recently to tell me that the bishop's son had sat across the table from their son Jacob at a scout banquet and after eyeing him for some time blurted out, "What's wrong with you, anyway?" Without hesitating, Jacob said, "I have Down syndrome, and Heavenly Father knows it—what's *your* problem?" Both mothers had to suppress a smile.

Far Different Places
Words and music by Janice Kapp Perry

A husband, a wife, a simple plan for life—
Love in our home, a child of our own
Then a lullaby tune from a hospital room
As hushed voices whispered the news
Just a simple exchange, yet everything changed
And I think in that moment we knew

Chorus
    Our journey would take us
    To far different places
    Than we had ever dreamed
    Our journey would take us
    To sad, lonely places
    That some have never seen
    Places with a different kind of beauty
    A special place apart
    Touching far different places in our hearts

A woman, a man, a very diff'rent plan—
Blessings to earn, and so much to learn

For this child of our love entrusted to us
Would help us be all we could be
God made no mistake, and though our hearts ached,
He touched us and helped us to see

Repeat Chorus

Bridge
So now we dream much smaller dreams
Finding joy in simple things
A word, a smile, can lift us up so high
Sometimes we laugh, sometimes we cry
But even in the sweetest times
We've come to realize

Repeat Chorus

❖   ❖   ❖

The Promise

I wrote lyrics for only two of the songs on the album we recorded for families with disabled members. In writing "The Promise," I was remembering a tender story I had read in the *Ensign* a few years before. It was true, and was written by the father of a young woman with Down syndrome.

The father had a dream one day about something that happened in our premortal life. He was with a group of people who were preparing for earth life, when the person in charge asked who among those present would be willing to come to earth with severe handicaps. In his mind he felt unwilling to volunteer, but while he was considering it, a beautiful young woman raised her hand and said, "I'll do it."

The man was so touched by her willing spirit that he immediately raised his hand and said (I'm paraphrasing), "If *she* is willing to do it, please let *me* be the one assigned to care for her and protect her and help her to return safely."

He felt the dream, or vision, was sent to help him gain understanding and insight into his daughter's spirit and to strengthen him for the task of doing what he had committed to do in her behalf.

In my interviews with parents of handicapped or disabled children, I heard of many similar spiritual experiences that seemed to have been given to parents to strengthen them for the day-to-day struggles that can sometimes feel overwhelming.

The Promise
Words and music by Janice Kapp Perry

In that place before our birth
Did you volunteer to come to earth
With many special trials to overcome
And when that choice was made
Did I raise my hand in perfect faith
And plead to have and hold you as my own
Did I promise I would lead you safely home?

Chorus
> Back home to love and light
> Where heaven's blessings are assured
> Back home to walk with angels
> In the presence of the Lord

Now we struggle here on earth
Trying hard to hear God's guiding word
And wonder if He's left us on our own
Then softly through the veil
Comes a feeling that I know so well
Because I knew you could not walk alone
I promised I would lead you safely home

Repeat Chorus

Then on some bright future day
Will I see things in a diff'rent way
When I remember who you really are
And will I come to see
That you paved the way to heaven for me
By helping me to grow and overcome
Did you know that you were leading me back home?

Repeat Chorus

Where we can be together
In glory yet unknown
Because we brought each other safely home

❖   ❖   ❖

I Will Heed the Word of God

Shortly after I joined the Mormon Tabernacle Choir in 1993, I met a wonderful couple on the staff there, Robert and Vy Morris. During my second year with the Choir they were called as full-time missionaries to Samoa. Before they left I said, "If you need music for any special occasion, just let me know."

Teaching music was the main thrust of their mission, in the schools as well as the Church. They soon organized a large and enthusiastic young adult choir and wrote to me requesting a song on the theme of heeding the word of God. The Morrises mentioned that the young people there were surrounded with many temptations and opportunities to stray from the teachings of the Church. They wanted a song that would reinforce their determination to remain true to the faith.

I based the song on Nephi's powerful words (1 Nephi 15:25): "Yea, I did exhort them with all the energies of my soul . . . that they would give heed to the word of God and remember to keep his commandments always in all things."

I was not able to hear the choir sing, but I heard glowing reports from the Morrises about their enthusiastic performances of the song on several occasions.

I Will Heed the Word of God
Words and music by Janice Kapp Perry

I am a disciple of Christ
Called out of the world into His light
Baptized in His name
I am not ashamed
To stand for His truth and light

I am a disciple of Christ
Endowed with the Spirit's perfect light
My pathway is clear
I've nothing to fear
If I do not compromise

Refrain
   I will heed the word of God
   I will live by every precept He has taught
   I will always safely trust
   In His saving words of love
   My heart and soul on Calvary He bought
   I will heed the word of God

I am a disciple of Christ
Sent forth as a light in latter days
And I will proclaim
The Lord's sacred name
And walk in His proven ways

I am a disciple of Christ
I'll serve Him through all my mortal life
My voice I will raise
His name I will praise
For His wond'rous sacrifice

Repeat Refrain

And though the world may try to tempt me
From the straight and narrow path
I will stand in strength and honor
Seeking all the Father hath

Repeat Refrain

❖   ❖   ❖

Love Can Make a Difference

My friends from the Tabernacle Choir, Robert and Vy Morris, completed their mission to Samoa and returned home to spend a little time with their family in Salt Lake City. Very soon, however, I received a letter from them from Tonga, where they were serving another mission! As usual, they were heavily involved in music education and had formed a choir that was to perform for various Church and community events.

I was pretty sure I knew what was coming next—a request for a song written especially for the Tongan Saints. This time the subject was love—always a favorite subject to ponder—and I was more than happy to accept the assignment.

At the end of our Savior's ministry it seemed almost as though He feared His disciples would not remember all He had taught them, so He summed things up with the oft-repeated admonition to "love one another, as I have loved you." Truly loving, as Jesus did, is the key to ministering as He did, and that message has been successfully passed down from Jesus' time to our own. I have experienced this as caring Church leaders have loved and supported us through trials in the same way I know Jesus would have.

It seemed especially appropriate to write this song for the Saints of Tonga, whose capacity for love is legendary.

Love Can Make a Difference
Words and music by Janice Kapp Perry

As if He feared they would not remember
All that He had spoken
Jesus turned to His disciples once again
His hour drew near and He spoke as one
Whose heart would soon be broken
Gentle words that touch us now as they did then
He said, "Love one another as I have loved you"
Love one another as you have seen me do

Refrain
    Love can make a diff'rence
    Love can make things right
    When the world seems cold and lonely
    Love can bring the light

The world cries out for a kind and caring
Hand to ease life's sorrows
Where is love to help and heal the human race?

God hears our prayers and He looks for
Willing hands that He may borrow
Hands to act as gentle angels in His place
We must love one another as He has loved us
Love one another, yes, love as Jesus does

Repeat Refrain

I am but one, but I'll heed the gentle
Whisp'rings of His Spirit
Sharing love with every brother in my way
When hearts cry out, I will try within
My willing heart to hear it
Every prompting from above I will obey
We must love one another as He has loved us
Love one another, yes, love as Jesus does

Jesus showed us the way
Jesus taught us to love
If we remember only this
Perhaps it is enough
Remember love

Repeat Refrain

Love can bring the light

❖   ❖   ❖

Thy Holy House

In 1996 Doug and I traveled to the Portland, Oregon, area to speak at two stake Relief Society conferences on Friday and Saturday and in a sacrament meeting on Sunday morning. We were housed in a nice motel within walking distance of the Portland temple.

Very early Sunday morning, before Doug awakened, I put on my walking shoes and clothes and began the mile walk to the temple. The road wound through a lush green wooded area. Suddenly I rounded the curve and caught my first view of that magnificent building. Except for a man in the security booth, who said good morning as I entered the grounds, I was completely alone.

The beauty there was surreal as the early morning sun shone on thousands of colorful dew-covered tulips and other spectacular flowers and greenery. The silence, except for a few soothing sounds of nature, was electrifying. The depth of my feelings caught me quite unaware. I could not hold back tears of joy as I circled the temple and observed scene after scene of nature's beauties, which I have never since been able to adequately describe.

Finally, I found a place just to sit and contemplate the majesty of the temple and to consider the significance of all that transpires there. It was not a day when I could go inside, but the experience somehow felt complete and fulfilling anyway. I felt my heart constrict with the joy of being there and feeling what I was feeling.

Words came into my mind as strongly as I have ever felt them come—"Lord, as I look upon thy holy house, I know I stand on hallowed ground." More and then more words came. I had no pencil or paper, and I prayed I would remember them. Reluctantly I left the grounds to return to the motel where I could record the words. By the time I reached the motel I had finished the first verse of a hymn I titled "Thy Holy House." The music was in my mind also, and I sang that first verse a cappella as part of my sacrament meeting talk later that morning. Verses 2 and 3 were written in later quiet times as I remembered that glorious experience.

This hymn was sung by a combined institute choir in the opening session of the October 1999 general conference, following President Gordon B. Hinckley's remarks about the temples that were under construction.

Thy Holy House
Words and music by Janice Kapp Perry

Lord, as I look upon Thy holy house
I know I stand on hallowed ground
My soul is lifted up to higher thoughts
With nature's beauty all around

And as I contemplate Thy wond'rous plan
Unfolded here within these walls
I speak a prayer of thanks within my heart
And tears of gratitude now fall

Lord, as I look upon Thy holy house
With heaven's blessings held in store
I joy in every sacred ordinance
Performed for those who've gone before
And as I ponder solemn covenants
Made here within this house of peace
I long, with worthy Saints, to enter in
This place where earth and heaven meet

Lord, as I look upon Thy holy house
Whose spires ascend to heav'n above
I sense the vastness of eternity
I feel the greatness of Thy love
And when I think of earthly families
Sealed here for all eternity
I feel assurance then of lasting joy
And endless happiness with Thee

❖   ❖   ❖

Today I Will Be Baptized

I have written several baptism songs for children through the years, songs in which I have tried to capture the feelings I experienced on my own baptism day. I still remember that experience clearly. The first verse recalls the teachings of my own mother, Ruth Kapp, leading up to my baptism. Verse 2 reflects my memory of my father, Jacob Kapp, placing his hands on my head to bestow the gift of the Holy Ghost.

I had received a request to write a baptism song for Gina Rawlinson from North Carolina. The baptism of our eldest grandchild, Jessica Perry, was also approaching. Doug and I were on a plane traveling to one of our speaking assignments when the idea for the song came. I had nothing to write on so I grabbed the little white air-sickness bag and scribbled the words on it. Later at the motel I rewrote it on more appropriate paper.

I was not able to attend Gina's baptism, but it was a sweet moment when I saw Jessie dressed in white for her baptism. I led those who attended in singing this song.

Today I Will Be Baptized
Words and music by Janice Kapp Perry

Today I make a choice to follow Jesus
To always try to live my life for Him
Today I promise willingly
To love and serve Him faithfully
Today I take upon me His dear name

And soon I will receive a gift from Father
The Holy Ghost to help me choose the right
As hands are placed upon my head
And sacred priesthood words are said
That I might have the Spirit's guiding light

Today there's wonder in my eyes
Today I will be baptized

❖   ❖   ❖

A Song of the Heart

For more than a decade, Doug and I have traveled to stakes throughout the Church to speak, primarily at stake Relief Society conferences. Unless the stake provided us with a theme, we entitled our presentation "A Song of the Heart," based on the well-known scripture that states "a song of the heart is a prayer unto God" (D&C 25:12). Under that heading we have been able to speak and sing on many gospel topics pertinent to women— giving service, developing talents, living a Christ-centered life, enduring our trials, and so forth.

In 1997 a stake Relief Society president invited us to speak in her stake. When I gave her the title "A Song of the Heart," she said, "Oh, that's *nice!* Send the song ahead to us, and we'll have a Relief Society chorus prepare it for your program." I told her I had not written a song on that subject, and she said, "Well, why haven't you?"—a good question for which I had no good answer! I determined right then and there to write such a song and send it to them in time for their chorus to prepare it.

There is always a little extra motivation for writing when you know it will culminate in a performance. In the lyrics I tried to describe the subtle song of the heart that constantly plays inside me.

Their performance of the song was all I could have hoped for, and I was left to wonder why I hadn't written the song years before. I have heard it scores of times at conferences since then, and it is the title song for an album I recorded (vocally) for my posterity—a true act of bravery.

A Song of the Heart
Words and music by Janice Kapp Perry

With each sunrise comes the promise of a beautiful new day
A gift from God to fill with mem'ries sweet
I awaken in the presence of the ones I truly love
My cup is full, it brings me to my knees
But there are no words to thank Him fittingly
Only the song of love that plays inside of me

Chorus
   For the song of the heart is a prayer unto God
   In each song of the heart the love of God is expressed
   Yes, a song of the heart is a prayer unto God
   And will be answered with a blessing on my head

With each sunset I reflect upon the wonders of my day
My heart is touched by beauty I have seen
I've been strengthened by each test and trial designed to help me grow
And so, once more, I fall upon my knees
But there are no words to thank Him fittingly
Only the song of love that plays inside of me

Repeat Chorus

As each song of my heart ascends to God above
May He hear in each one the song of redeeming love

Repeat Chorus

Every song of the heart, every song of the heart
Is a prayer unto God

❖   ❖   ❖

As a Mother

A short time after Craig Jessop was appointed associate director of the Mormon Tabernacle Choir, he approached me about writing a Mother's Day song for the Choir. The Choir had sung a few of my Primary songs, but this was my first assignment to write something specifically for them. I was overjoyed! Craig's next words were, "Please don't write something that will make all the mothers feel guilty or my wife will have my head!" I knew exactly what he meant—I've felt that way too.

I thought about the song for some time but delayed writing it. Finally, at what I thought was the last minute, I went to our cabin for two days to think, pray, and write without interruption. I wrote two Mother's Day songs, hoping one of them would be right for the Choir.

My inclination was to write a separate verse about three mothers from the scriptures who inspire me: Eve, mother of all living; Sarah, mother of the nations; and Mary, mother of the Savior. After describing their significant accomplishments I expressed my personal desire as a mother in our day to stand with Mary, Sarah, and Eve, knowing there is no greater joy I may receive than knowing I have helped in quiet ways "from my sweet eternal place as a mother."

I submitted the song to Brother Jessop, but I had misunderstood the deadline, and it was too late for Mother's Day 1997 programming. I contented myself that I had at least finally written a Mother's Day song, something I had meant to do for years. I was so pleased when "As a Mother" was included a year later in the Choir's 1998 Mother's Day broadcast. I heard that Sister Jessop approved, which made *my* day!

As a Mother

Words and music by Janice Kapp Perry

Eve, mother of all living,
Commanded to replenish the earth
A gift of infinite worth
Mother of all living
And who am I
A mother in our day
So eager to achieve
The faith of mother Eve
As I follow one who blessed the human race
I will celebrate my place as a mother

Sarah, mother of the nations,
Bore Isaac in the twilight of life
Revered as Abraham's wife
Mother of the nations
And who am I
But mother of a few
Like Sarah, I believe
The legacy I leave
Will shine in ways that time cannot erase
And will sanctify my place as a mother

Mary, mother of the Savior,
A handmaid who obeyed the Lord's will
And nations honor her still
Mother of the Savior
And who am I
A mother filled with love
And I, like Mary, know
That as my children grow
And learn as Jesus did, from grace to grace,
They will magnify my place as a mother

I stand with Mary, with Sarah, and with Eve
Knowing there is no greater joy I may receive
No riches, no words of earthly praise
Are like knowing I have helped in quiet ways
From my sweet, eternal place as a mother

❖   ❖   ❖

Coming Home

For everyone, there is a sweet remembered place that we call home. For me, that place is the small farming community of Vale, Oregon, where I attended grade school, junior high, and high school. There I played ball, dated, danced, attended church, and grew up under the loving tutelage of my parents, Jacob and Ruth Kapp. There "the music of my soul was formed and fashioned and the rhythm of my life was first begun." The mention of that obscure little community always evokes tender feelings, though I have not lived there since 1961.

In 1997, as the Church celebrated 150 years since the arrival of the pioneers in the Salt Lake Valley, Church leaders in Vale, Oregon, planned a grand sesquicentennial reunion for everyone who had ever lived in the Vale Ward. Plans were made a year in advance, and word spread far and wide of the coming event. I knew for certain I wanted to be part of it. As we made plans to attend, I pondered an appropriate way to express my feelings about growing up there. A song seemed the best way.

Writing the song was an emotional experience. My father died in 1970 and my mother in 1991, and returning to Vale always caused my mind to be flooded with memories of them. "I see my father's face in each green acre, And I hear my mother's voice in morning sounds."

More than one thousand people attended the reunion. There was a corn-and-watermelon feed at the church, a picnic in the park, a talent show at my old high school, a Sunday morning church service at the high school, and time for lots of visiting and reflection. I was grateful there was music to express the feelings that were a little too deep for words alone, as I sang "Coming Home" to my friends.

Coming Home
Words and music by Janice Kapp Perry

Within my heart there is a sweet remembered place that I call home
A quiet place with mem'ries time cannot erase though years have flown
A place where childhood days were filled with love and faith
That gave me strength to go out on my own

And though I've traveled far upon this earth
The things of greatest worth I learned at home

Chorus
    Coming home is like walking through a gate
    In my mind, to a sweet familiar place
    Where I see my father's face in each green acre
    And I hear my mother's voice in morning sounds
    And even though they're gone
    The feelings linger on
    And that's the joy of coming home

Through all the years I have recalled
The joy that blessed my childhood home
And loving friends who walked beside me until I could stand alone
A place so dear to me that it will always be
The time and place where seeds of life were sown

With memories of love still burning bright
There's really nothing quite like coming home

Repeat Chorus

Where the music of my soul was formed and fashioned
And the rhythm of my life was first begun
And though the years have passed
The mem'ries seem to last
And that's the joy of coming home

❖   ❖   ❖

Everyday Heroes

In 1997 Senator Orrin Hatch and I had nearly completed writing our first album of patriotic songs. There was room for one more song on the recording, and we were searching for just the right idea.

In April that year I performed with the Tabernacle Choir at a special convocation at Southern Utah University in Cedar City. Former president George Bush was the keynote speaker. His speech was dynamic and touching as he told the stories of several "everyday heroes" in our nation who had made a positive difference in their neighborhoods, and often far beyond, by giving their time, means, and hearts to worthwhile projects. He had my full attention as I enjoyed each inspiring story. Suddenly the light went on in my mind as I realized he had given us the title for our final song: "Everyday Heroes."

As soon as the choir returned home that day I called the senator at his Virginia home and said, "George Bush gave us our final song title!" He loved the idea, too, and went right to work on the words. The result was a lively, upbeat song that has had many performances throughout the country, has been published by several music companies throughout the nation, and performed by scores of high school choirs. In April 1999 nine thousand high school chorus members from all over the United States performed it at the Washington Monument in Washington, D.C., as part of the *America Sings* festival. I attended the program and found it extremely moving.

George and Barbara Bush were kind enough to give a strong endorsement of our patriotic album.

Everyday Heroes
Words by Senator Orrin Hatch
Music by Janice Kapp Perry

Some people have eyes to see
A friend in need of help
They love to reach out to those
Who cannot help themselves

Some people have ears to hear
The cries of those in need
They show us how much they care
Through quiet simple deeds

Chorus
> Everyday heroes
> Live in every neighborhood.
> Everyday heroes
> Helping in the way neighbors should
> Giving just a little time
> Sharing just a little love
> God bless each one of those
> Everyday heroes

Some people have helping hands
That go the second mile
They're willing to love and lift
A brother for a while

Some people have hearts that feel
The hopelessness of men
They're willing to walk with them
Until they're strong again.

Repeat Chorus

Bridge
    Teach a child to read, help a friend in need
    Mend a broken fence or a broken heart
    Plant a flow'r or two, give a part of you—
    That's how it starts!

Repeat Chorus

❖   ❖   ❖

Heal Our Land

During the summer of 1996 I attended the funeral of my cousin Judy Lester in Brigham City, Utah. Before the service I was introduced to Senator Orrin Hatch, whose youngest daughter, Kim, had married Judy's youngest brother, John Catron, several years earlier.

I was pleased to meet the senator, whom I had admired for many years. As we shook hands he said, "I enjoy your music very much—I write poetry, you know." I had not known that, but casually answered, "Well, we should collaborate some time." Responding with an intensity that surprised me, he said, "Yes, we really should! When can we discuss this?"

I left the funeral wondering if he had been serious, but I soon received a call from Washington, D.C., following up on the idea. Before long I traveled with the Tabernacle Choir to Washington, and the Hatches invited Doug and me to one of Elaine's delicious Sunday dinners. After dinner the senator showed me several impressive volumes of poetry he had written through the years—on both secular and religious themes. We then spent time discussing the differences between poetry and lyrics, and he expressed confidence that he could learn to write lyrics.

Upon my return to Utah, he began sending batches of lyrics—mostly hymn texts, to begin with. My first feeling about his writing was gratitude that someone representing us in Washington would have these spiritual thoughts in his mind and heart. I set many of those first hymns to music, though he was a bit too prolific for me to keep up with his pace.

I will always remember the day when I opened an envelope from the senator and saw a page of lyrics entitled "Heal Our Land." Coming at a time when President Bill Clinton was bringing dishonor and divisiveness to our country, I thrilled at the title and read the words eagerly. When I did so I had a strong feeling that it was an important song that would have a far-reaching effect on our country.

I made it a matter of prayer before I began writing the music and felt the Spirit confirm my initial feeling about its importance. We decided to subtitle the song "A Prayer for Our Country."

In the years following publication, this piece has been recorded by us and by others, has been performed by several symphony orchestras and choruses, has been performed at two National Prayer Breakfasts, has been published in choral form by national publishers, and seems to be rolling on to the national prominence I foresaw when I first saw the senator's lyrics. I truly believe in the power of music to help heal our land. I hope this offering may help in that process.

Heal Our Land

Words by Senator Orrin Hatch
Music by Janice Kapp Perry

Heal our land
Please grant us peace today
And strengthen all who lack the faith
To call on Thee each day
Heal our land
And keep us safe and free
Watch over all who understand
The need for liberty

Chorus
>   Heal our land, heal our land
>   And guide us with Thy hand
>   Keep us ever on the path of liberty
>   Heal our land, heal our land
>   And help us understand
>   That we must put our trust in Thee
>   If we would be free

Heal our land
Please help us find our way
For in Thy word we find our strength
If we look up each day
Heal our land
And fill us with Thy love
Keep us upon the path of truth
That comes from heaven above.

Repeat Chorus

Protect us by the power of Thy rod
And keep us as one nation under God

Repeat Chorus

❖ ❖ ❖

Freedom's Light

After I began my collaboration with Senator Orrin Hatch in earnest, I encouraged him to concentrate on patriotic themes for a time. "Freedom's Light" may have been the first set of patriotic lyrics he sent. I looked at the page that contained twenty-eight lines and thought, "There are some wonderful lines there, but it isn't quite right yet." I was a little timid at first about suggesting changes to this highly respected statesman but carefully brought up the idea during a telephone conversation.

"Of course," he said. "We're collaborators—that means we work together for the best result!" Looking at the lyrics later that day, in a prayerful frame of mind, I could see the whole song was there if the order of the lines was altered rather dramatically. I looked at the sheet and could suddenly see the form and order clearly. It was an unusual and profound experience. I had the feeling that the Lord loves Orrin Hatch, because I feel His guidance when I work with him.

Powerful lines abound in this piece, but I especially appreciate these lines from the chorus: "We'll feed the fire of freedom's flame, we'll keep our dream alive, so this blessed land may always feel the glow of heaven's light."

The considerable talents of arranger Greg Hansen and vocalist Paul Engemann made this a powerful and exciting title song on our *Freedom's Light* recording.

Freedom's Light
Words by Senator Orrin Hatch
Music by Janice Kapp Perry

In this dark day of discontent
So many feel despair
As poverty and dissidence
Cause sadness everywhere
But through it all the patriot's dream
Lives on in yearning hearts
For we believe in freedom's theme
Which God, Himself, imparts

Chorus
> This land, the arc of freedom's light,
> Is home to you and me
> And we must keep it burning bright
> From sea to shining sea
> We'll feed the fire of freedom's flame
> We'll keep our dream alive
> So this blessed land may always feel
> The glow of freedom's light

So many say our glory days
Will never be again
And angry voices undermine
The works of honest men
But God above will strengthen us
If valiant hearts unite

We'll raise our voice in freedom's song
We'll walk in freedom's light!

Repeat Chorus

Bridge
   Some have died for freedom's cause
   Heroes in the fight
   Who gave their all because they saw
   The power of freedom's light

Repeat Chorus

❖   ❖   ❖

I Stand with Jesus Christ

Ours is truly a worldwide Church now. After a choral performance of the song I wrote for the Samoan Saints ("I Will
Heed the Word of God"), Elder and Sister Morris were
approached by Peter and Joyce Chen, visitors to Samoa from
Hong Kong. They expressed to the Morrises the wish that I
might write a song for the Saints of Hong Kong also. Sister
Morris passed the request along to me, saying, "I didn't promise
anything. I just said I would ask."

My interest was immediate. It was a time of uncertainty for
the Hong Kong Saints because their country was to revert to
China the next year. I wanted very much to write a meaningful
song for them but was unsure how to approach it. That very
month I read an article in the *Ensign* about the Saints in Hong
Kong. As I read, the theme of the song became obvious. Those
who were interviewed said that regardless of changes that might
occur, they would find safety and strength by standing with
Jesus Christ, obeying His commandments, and keeping the
covenants made in their new temple. The title "I Stand with Jesus
Christ" seemed perfect, and I added a flavor of Chinese music
to the accompaniment. I sent the piece to the Chens, who had
by this time returned to Hong Kong.

I also entered the piece in the Church's Relief Society song-
writing contest. It was one of the winners and was performed

by a chorus at the BYU Women's Conference under the direction of Dyanne Riley in 1998.

In August 1999 I met a Brother Bohn on BYU campus. He said he had been the first to perform the piece in Hong Kong while serving as a missionary and that the Saints had adopted it and perpetuated it through many performances. I also met the Chens, who came to Provo, and they confirmed its acceptance by the Hong Kong Saints—a fact that pleased me greatly.

I Stand with Jesus Christ

Words and music by Janice Kapp Perry

Winds of change are all around me
Feel it now, in the air
Whispers of the world surround me
Calling here, calling there

Where is something I can hold onto
Something sure, something true?
Lord of all creation, strengthen me
Keep me safe with thee

Refrain
> I stand with Jesus Christ,
> He fills my soul with light
> Kingdoms may fall
> Men may build walls
> But He ruleth over all
> I feel my Savior's love
> His Spirit bears me up
> Storms may arise
> Blinding men's eyes
> But I stand with Jesus Christ

Voices of confusion linger
Hear them now, everywhere
Some may weaken and may wonder
Is God real, does He care?

Lord in heaven, please look down on me
Help me stay close to thee
Let me see that through the winds of change
Truth and light remain

Repeat Refrain

Holy temples stand in latter days
Making sure heaven's ways
Prophets testify and speak His will
God is with us still

Repeat Refrain

I stand with Jesus Christ

❖   ❖   ❖

Legacy

I wrote "Legacy," a Mother's Day song, during the same two days when I wrote "As a Mother." In this one, I expressed all the wonderful, loving feelings I have for my own mother, who died just a few years before I wrote the song. I can never adequately explain how powerfully she influenced my life for good. "Everything that she held dear, is also dear to me, There is so much of Mother in me."

The song then explores the other seasons of life—becoming mother in my mother's place as she moved on to grandmother. Now, as a grandmother myself, I enjoy watching as my children and their children pass along the timeless legacy that I received from my mother, and she from hers, and on and on.

Legacy
Words and music by Janice Kapp Perry

I remember Mother
And now I understand
Through all the days of childhood
My life was in her hands
For everything that she held dear
Is also dear to me
There is so much of Mother in me

Time has passed so quickly
I'm mother in her place
With children who are learning

The truths they will embrace
And as I watch them find their way
It humbles me to see
There is so much they're learning from me

Bridge
  The gifts we give our children
  Are gifts they'll someday share
  For all their hopes and all their dreams
  Are fashioned by our care

Now that I am grandma
I often think I see
My children's children living
A timeless legacy
And in my heart I know
They're part of one eternal round
Where a love through the ages is found
To which hearts of the children are bound

❖   ❖   ❖

Many Different Roads

The year 1997 brought the deaths of two well-known women of our time who were diverse in almost every aspect of their lives and yet united in their impulse toward charity—Princess Diana and Mother Teresa.

One was tall, the other short; one was old, the other young; one was rich, the other poor; one was before the cameras her whole life, the other shunned the camera. Yet each had the capacity for unjudging sympathy. A few months before their deaths, Diana paid a visit to the nun whose devotion to the poor and dying she was beginning to absorb. Though both the "Saint of the Gutters" and "Princess of the People" walked very different roads, each made a unique contribution to the human race.

Every magazine on the stands was filled with fascinating information about the lives of these two women. Writers spoke of the stark contrast between their two lives but noted their common attraction toward lifting hurting humanity. It was an interesting subject for a song, and I began to write ideas from my reading into a set of lyrics I entitled "Many Different Roads." Knowing my friend Orrin Hatch had been acquainted with Mother Teresa, I invited him to join me in writing the lyrics. We both felt satisfaction from this project, and it helped quiet my sad feelings over the loss of these two significant humanitarians. We released the song on a CD single.

Just before the song was released, I received a letter from Jimmy Newman, son of Gladys Knight (of Gladys Knight and the Pips fame), saying that Gladys had recently been baptized into the LDS Church and was soliciting demo tapes for an album of gospel music she was planning. I sent him a few of my best-known songs and, almost as an afterthought, included a rough studio version of "Many Different Roads." A few weeks later we were delighted to hear Gladys Knight had chosen this piece as the title song for her first gospel album. Adding a few words of her own, and subtracting a few of ours to make room, she released her *Many Different Roads* album in 1998.

Orrin Hatch and I released our original version of "Many Different Roads" in 1998 on our album *Jesus' Love Is like a River.*

Many Different Roads

Words by Janice Kapp Perry and Senator Orrin Hatch
Music by Janice Kapp Perry

Princess Diana
Born to privilege and wealth
Moved in lofty circles, yet found within herself
The will to walk among the sad and lonely
And lift them with a smile or tender gaze
She for whom true joy was so elusive
Gave her love to strangers in her way
Her final ride through somber streets of London
Brought tears and grief the world has never seen
This princess who was champion of the lowly
In the hearts of all the world became a queen

Many different roads can lead to glory
Many different lamps can bring the light
In majesty she walked in humble places
Her common touch a candle in the night

Mother Teresa
With humility and grace
Gave her life to healing the hurting human race
She saw in them the gentle face of Jesus
And lifted them to dignity and peace
Her worn and weathered face smiled on the children
Bringing hope unto the least of these
Her final ride through streets of old Calcutta
A moving scene no artist's brush could paint
This humble soul who lived her life for Jesus
In the hearts of all the world is now a saint

Many different roads can lead to glory
Many different paths a saint may walk
In poverty she shared a wealthy spirit
And helped the poor to see the face of God

Bridge

A princess and a pauper
Walked the lonely roads of life
In many ways so different
And yet so much alike

Many different roads can lead to glory
Many different lamps can bring the light
Both rich and poor may write a golden story
That shines through time like candles in the night

❖   ❖   ❖

On Wings of Song

Many times I have received comfort from music that seemed heaven sent for a sad occasion. When my grandfather Reuben Saunders died while I was attending BYU, I was comforted completely as I heard "Oh My Father" sung at his funeral. That same experience has been repeated at many succeeding family funerals—I remember the music long after the sermons have faded from memory.

When my own father was dying at age fifty-seven, he asked that Mother keep playing the organ and piano in their home because he found it very comforting. Two days after his funeral I turned on my car radio and heard the Tabernacle Choir offer these calming words of explanation: "In my Father's house are many mansions, I go to prepare a place for you." My tears flowed freely in a way that brought a measure of understanding and peace. I cannot even begin to count the times I have felt heaven send its healing, "born softly on the wings of song."

My daughter, Lynne, and I were asked to speak and sing at the BYU Women's Conference in 1997 on how music sustains us in times of trial. I wrote the words to "On Wings of Song" for that occasion, and she and I sang it in an a cappella duet to begin our presentation. The tune is an old Appalachian gospel melody, author unknown.

On Wings of Song
Words by Janice Kapp Perry
Appalachian Gospel Tune

There will be days of sorrow
And moments of great doubt and fear
There may be clouds tomorrow
And often times for tender tears
Where may I turn for solace
Where shall I look to find my peace
And when I long for comfort
Where will my troubled heart find ease

Refrain
    Then comes a sound so soothing
    A harmony serene and calm
    As heaven sends its healing
    Borne softly on the wings of song

There will be days of sorrow
A time to weep, a time to mourn
Where may I fortune borrow
And courage to withstand the storm
There is a time for silence
Far from the pain of my distress

When Spirit gives me guidance
A time for sweet renewing rest

Repeat Refrain

With every soft vibration
Each melody that bears me up
I, from my lowly station,
Am lifted to the throne of love

Repeat Refrain

❖   ❖   ❖

One Nation under God

Senator Orrin Hatch and I chose this beautiful and meaningful phrase from the Pledge of Allegiance as one of our patriotic song titles. So many in our nation are forgetting that this
country was founded under God's divine guidance and will
endure only if we acknowledge our dependence on Him. Many,
in fact, would have us become a godless society.

When we began our patriotic album project, I asked the senator, "In so many situations now we are told to be careful about
mentioning God, prayer, and religion. What will your stand be
on this album—are you willing to openly declare our country's
need to be one nation under God?"

With all the passion of his heart and soul he answered that
he would never hold back or equivocate in any way on that
subject, that he would boldly proclaim our nation's dependence
on God every chance he got. Every set of lyrics he has written
has borne out this statement, and I greatly admire his integrity
in this important matter.

One Nation under God
Words by Senator Orrin Hatch
Music by Janice Kapp Perry

America has welcomed all
From many distant lands

Brave pilgrims seeking liberty
Who crossed the water in God's hands
  Every honest freedom-seeking soul
  America has welcomed all

The heart and might of this great land
Is found in our beliefs
Our faith that God's unfailing hand
Will help preserve our liberties
  And we invite all men who gather here
  To worship God . . . and feel no fear

Chorus
  When we are one nation under God
  Our freedoms will endure
  One nation under God
  Whose promises are sure
  He will bless and keep our land
  Safe by His almighty hand
  This is the hope for which men fought—
  One nation under God

We'll sing the song of liberty
With voices strong and clear
We'll seek for God's protecting care
Upon this land that we hold dear
  For He will guide us through our darkest hour
  If we will trust His sovereign power

Repeat Chorus

❖   ❖   ❖

Jesus' Love Is like a River

Senator Orrin Hatch usually sends several sets of lyrics at a time and asks that I extract the "gems" and set them to music. As I sifted through one such batch of lyrics, I was dazzled by the simple but profound images in "Like a River." I couldn't wait to write the music.

Phrases such as these touched me deeply: "Jesus' love is like a river running gently through my soul," or "Jesus' love is like the sunshine falling softly on my face," or "Jesus' love is like a lighthouse when the storms of life appear." To read these words that even approximated the great love I feel for my Savior, made my heart constrict with joy and tears come to my eyes. I hoped to write music to match his eloquent lyrics.

The song has been recorded by Felicia Sorenson (on our album *Jesus' Love Is like a River*), by Santita Jackson (Rev. Jesse Jackson's daughter), and by Gladys Knight (on her debut gospel album, *Many Different Roads*). I have sung it at scores of firesides and on my own vocal album, *A Song of the Heart*. The message always moves me with its beautiful imagery.

I received an unusual response to this song after a speech I gave to some women at BYU in the spring of 2000. An older woman approached me, trembling with emotion as she related her story. Decades earlier a car in which she was riding with her mother and little brother left the road and became submerged in a body of water. Her mother and brother drowned in the accident, but she was rescued in time. All these years later she could still recall the terror of that experience and, understandably, has retained a terrible fear of water. She said she cried as I sang "Like a River" because for the first time she had a new feeling about water—that it can be gentle, soothing, and peaceful. She hoped it would help her overcome a lifelong phobia.

I am constantly amazed at the power of music to heal, comfort, and inspire in so many diverse and unusual circumstances.

Jesus' Love Is like a River

Words by Senator Orrin Hatch
Music by Janice Kapp Perry

Jesus' love is like a river
Flowing gently through my soul
And the grace that it delivers
Makes me peaceful, makes me whole
For everything grows where the water goes
And everything lives where the water flows

Jesus' love is like a river
Flowing gently through my soul

Jesus' love is like the sunshine
Falling softly on my face
And it warms me like a fire
Bringing comfort, bringing peace
For everything grows where the sunlight goes
And everything's green where the sunlight glows
Jesus' love is like the sunshine
Falling softly on my face

Jesus' love is like a lighthouse
When the storms of life appear
Like a beacon in the distance—
Always steady, always clear
And those who will go where the lighthouse glows
Are warmed by His spirit and find repose
Jesus' love is like a lighthouse
When the storms of life appear

Jesus' love is like a river
Like the sunshine on my face
Jesus' love is like a lighthouse
Leading to His peaceful place

❖   ❖   ❖

Thy Word Is a Lamp unto My Feet

Five or six years ago I was reading from the book of Psalms
on a Sunday evening and was again touched by the poetic
phrases that abound in the scriptures. I was particularly drawn
to Psalm 119:105: "Thy word is a lamp unto my feet, and a light
unto my path." I marked it for future reference feeling that I
would love to set that beautiful phrase to music someday.

Several times in the ensuing years I revisited that idea but,
with no deadlines, I kept putting it off. In 1997 I received a
letter regarding the upcoming BYU Women's Conference in
which the leaders were soliciting essays on that very passage

of scripture. Winners would be chosen and the writers would be invited to present their essays at a session of the April Women's Conference.

I considered writing an essay, but as usual I was much more interested in conveying my ideas musically. I wasn't sure they would accept music when they were asking for essays, but it gave me a reason to finally write it, which I did, and sent it in. I was pleased when they responded with an invitation to have it performed in the middle of their essay-reading session. I later entered it in the Relief Society song-writing contest, with good results.

There is a special spiritual connection with an audience when the words of the scriptures are set to music (I once read the Book of Mormon from cover to cover just to mark scriptures that could be set to music—now if I can just live long enough!). The idea of the Lord's word lighting our uncertain path in mortality is so comforting to me because, as is stated in that same section of Psalms, "I have inclined my heart to perform [His] statutes alway, even unto the end" (119:112).

Thy Word Is a Lamp unto My Feet
Words and music by Janice Kapp Perry

I am a child, so far from home
Strangely adrift, yet not alone
I'm learning line on line
I'm growing grace by grace
Clinging to the light I have been given
Until I hear Thy voice
Until I see Thy face
Until I truly taste of heaven

Chorus
    "Thy word is a lamp unto my feet,
    And a light unto my path"
    It leads to the source of purest love
    And to all the Father hath
    It resounds in my soul
    Like a voice from long ago
    In words so pure and sweet
    "Thy word is a lamp unto my feet"

I pray to Thee each day for strength
To find and walk the narrow way
I left from one safe shore
And I'll return once more
Faithful to the truths I have been given
For in my heart I feel
Thy promises are real—
Thy light will lead me back to heaven

Repeat Chorus

Some day beyond the veil
I'll worship at Thy feet
But 'til that blessed day
When faith and knowledge meet

Repeat Chorus

❖   ❖   ❖

When Saints Unite to Sing God's Praise

In 1997, my husband felt a strong impression that I should devote some of my time to writing hymns. Specifically, he challenged me to write one hundred hymns! Initially I balked, feeling uncertain about my ability to write suitable hymn texts. But as if by design, I began receiving beautiful hymn texts from three different writers, and I found it very rewarding to give their texts musical settings. To date I have written seventy-one hymns and find it a very satisfying pursuit.

I have written only a few hymn texts myself. It seems I can only write a worthwhile text when I have had a significant spiritual experience. Perhaps it is that way for every writer of hymns—something must be deeply felt in order to ignite the spirit to produce something worthy.

On a quiet Sunday afternoon, several months before my retirement from the Tabernacle Choir, I was resting and pondering the great joy I felt every time I practiced or performed with the Choir. Knowing that my retirement was imminent (mandatory at age sixty), I felt a desire to write a hymn that would convey my feelings to my fellow Choir members and our directors.

The title came immediately to mind: "When Saints Unite to Sing God's Praise." Although I hadn't planned to write the hymn that very day, I could scarcely hold back the flow of ideas. All the joyous feelings I had experienced during my five years with the Choir seemed to spill onto the page in the next hour. In the evening I added the music and tweaked the words here and there. Then Doug typeset it for me. I felt a certain excitement and also relief from having given expression to these feelings. I sent a copy of the hymn to our director.

Brother Jerold Ottley informed me a few months later that the Choir would sing the hymn in the Sunday morning session of my final general conference and also the next Sunday on my final broadcast—a very kind gesture. Those two events were very tender for me, and the hymn provided a meaningful way for me to say good-bye to my Choir friends. I hope the hymn will be used in other ways in the future, but in my heart it will always be for the Tabernacle Choir.

When Saints Unite to Sing God's Praise
Words and music by Janice Kapp Perry

When Saints unite to sing God's praise
His Spirit will abound
As with one blended voice we raise
An anthem heaven bound
When in our worship we combine
To sing with one accord
In one grand chorus we define
Our rev'rence for the Lord

When words alone cannot convey
Vibrations of the heart
Sweet strains of sacred music may
Our noblest thoughts impart
The deepest joys of humankind
The raptures of the soul
Expand as joyful voices blend
In one harmonic whole

If in our hearts we consecrate
Our anthems to the Lord
The love of God shall resonate
In each resounding chord
When through our music we declare
Devotion to His word
Our song, ascending like a prayer
Shall reach the throne of God

❖   ❖   ❖

He Was Watching Over Me

Most of my life has been unusually peaceful and happy. Years ago I even found myself wondering why I didn't seem to have the serious tests and trials others had. And then out of the blue I experienced a series of traumatic events that made me wonder if I could ever be truly happy again.

It seemed that the harder I petitioned the Lord for understanding and peace of mind, the farther I felt from Him. I prayed for light and felt overcome by greater darkness. I have never felt so alone. It seemed as if the Lord had withdrawn His Spirit from me, which seemed unfair, as I felt I had done nothing to displease Him.

This struggle persisted over a few year's time. Eventually I became aware that the Lord was allowing me this painful experience to teach me things I could learn in no other way. And although my specific prayers were seemingly unanswered, He had spoken to me on two or three occasions unexpectedly and much more directly than at any other time in my life.

Only with the perspective of time have I come to understand that He was always watching over me, seeing things I could not see and answering in the timing He knew was best for my spiritual growth. When pride and will and hurt feelings were finally dissolved into a humble acceptance of His will, I was able to forgive what seemed unforgivable and emerge from darkness with greater light. "I guess He knew it all along, the things that hurt so much would make me strong—that in my hour of greatest need, I would turn to Him and let Him lead, knowing He was watching over me."

He Was Watching Over Me

Words and music by Janice Kapp Perry

I prayed for strength
He gave me weakness to make me strong
I prayed for light
He sent the darkness and hope seemed gone
At times I felt so all alone
As if He'd left me on my own
He didn't seem to see it was too much for me
But weakness turned to strength
And darkness turned to light
And looking back I see
He was with me through the fight

Refrain

> And He was watching over me
> Seeing what I could not see
> I guess He knew it all along
> The things that hurt so much
> Would make me strong
> That in my hour of greatest need
> I would turn to Him and let Him lead

I prayed for calm
He sent a tempest to make me bold
I prayed for sun
He sent a rainfall to cleanse my soul
I was a lamb out in the cold
Begging the Shepherd "bring me home"
Yet in my hour of need He hid His face from me
But tempest turned to calm
And rain has turned to sun
And looking back I see
He was with me all along

Repeat Refrain

Knowing He was watching over me

Livin' My Dream

The last decade or so of my life has been an exercise in over-coming fears—fears of speaking, fears of singing, fears of being in the public eye. After we recorded our first album in 1979, I received requests to speak before various groups, and I declined for two years. Finally I decided to try to overcome that fear, which took about five years. I didn't do any singing on these programs but depended on others to provide the music. Then I decided to overcome my fear of singing publicly, which took another few years.

Through the twenty years we have recorded albums of my songs, I have left the singing to the pros. Yet I have always har-bored a little dream that I would one day be brave enough to sing an album of songs myself, if only for my posterity. Turn-ing sixty and feeling my mortality a bit finally gave me the courage to do that in 1999.

I wrote "Livin' My Dream" specifically for the album and to sing at future firesides, at which I often speak about overcom-ing fears and developing new talents. I wish I had been braver a bit earlier, and I hope this song will encourage others to do just that!

Whatever the outcome of this recording, "I gave it my best, now I'll have no regrets—I'm livin' my dream."

Livin' My Dream
Words and music by Janice Kapp Perry

Do you have a dream, a wish deep inside you
An outrageous scheme, then until you have tried
You will never quite know just how far you can go
In livin' your dream

I had a dream, I think it's worth saying
I wanted to sing with an orchestra playing
A very bold choice for my average voice
But this was my dream

Chorus
    So I hired some strings and some woodwinds and things
    And a few shiny brass just to give it some class
    I decided to hire a fine back-up choir

Paid them all that I could to make me sound good
Then I wrote down a song
Something simple but strong
Hired someone to lead who could help me succeed
And I'm livin' my dream

So if you have a dream, don't hide or deny it
Just bravely decide to stand up and try it
You may be surprised after twenty-five tries
You'll be livin' your dream

I used to just dream, but now I am older
I risk a few things, I feel a bit bolder
If I want to try something pie in the sky
I'll follow that dream

Repeat Chorus

And someday, don't laugh, I may even aspire
To sing with the Mormon Tabernacle Choir!

This was my dream, just one of those things
I knew I must try, though I couldn't say why
So I gave it my best, now I'll have no regrets
I'm livin' my dream

❖   ❖   ❖

Perry Family Song

At the end of 1999 I fulfilled a dream I had had for a decade
or so—I chose an album's worth of songs that held special
meaning for me and personally recorded them with my children and grandchildren. Even Grandpa Doug sings three notes!
Most of the songs were spiritual in nature, so I lightened things
up a little with the "Perry Family Song."

This playful bluegrass rendition tells the story of our family
from 1958, when Doug and I were married, up to the present
time, when our family has expanded to twenty-two. Our children and grandchildren joined in on the recording just as they
have in every happy event in our lives.

Perry Family Song
Words and music by Janice Kapp Perry

1. When we first got married in '58
   I told the Lord I'd appreciate
   A few fine sons who could sing and act
   He gave me four, but He took one back

   > **A.** We're mama's boys, we're the back-up singers
   > We're mama's boys, we're the back-up choir

2. Well, I asked for a daughter to sing with me
   One with a knack for harmony
   I knew we could have ourselves some fun—
   He heard my prayer and He gave me one

   > **B.** Sing a little song with me in harmony
   > Sing a little song to make me smile

(Sing A & B combined)

3. When the boys got married to a singer or two
   Our family chorus just grew and grew
   Our daughter married more than a pretty face
   She found her a man with a fine, deep bass

   > **C.** Bm, bm, bm, bm — bm, bm, bm, bm
   > Bm, bm, bm, bm — bm, bm, bm, bm

(Sing A, B & C combined)

4. Well, the grandkids came and they sang along
   Their love for music was good and strong
   They were boys and girls who could feel a beat
   They clapped their hands and they sang so sweet

   > **D.** Clap, clap our hands, we got rhythm
   > Clap, clap our hands, we got style

(Sing A, B, C & D combined)

5. It's been forty years and it seems quite strange
   Grandpa says he's got just a three-note range
   So I wrote him a line that's simple and true
   He sings it to me, and says "I love you"

(Sing A, B, C & D combined)

6. Now we count our blessings and sing along
   We love the rhythm of our family song
   We'll all be singin' till the day we die
   When our heavenly choir will be multiplied:

(Sing A, B, C & D combined, then repeat once more)

INDEX